Gary O'Malley —

Northeast Asia in Prehistory

NORTHEAST
ASIA
IN
PREHISTORY

Chester S. Chard

*The University
of Wisconsin
Press*

Published 1974
The University of Wisconsin Press
Box 1379, Madison, Wisconsin 53701

The University of Wisconsin Press, Ltd.
70 Great Russell Street, London

First printing

Printed in the United States of America

For LC CIP information see the colophon

ISBN 0-299-06430-1

Contents

Illustrations

Maps

Preface

Northeast Asia in Prehistory was designed as a general survey of the current state of knowledge of human history, adaptation, and cultural development in this part of the world from the earliest traces of man down to the beginning of the historic period. The latter boundary varies from the early centuries of the Christian era (in the case of Korea) to scarcely 250 years ago (in the case of much of northern Siberia). The area covered comprises Siberia from the Altai Mountains and Yenisei River valley eastwards, Mongolia, Manchuria, Korea, and Japan. This area has a certain coherence. Geographically, if we except western Siberia with its close affinities to European Russia, it represents the steppe, forest, and tundra zones of northern Asia, lying beyond the loess farmland of traditional China. The area is one of independent hearths of culture, and historically is set off by a puzzling lack of Chinese influence in the period with which we are concerned. Siberia and adjacent regions are of course of great interest to New World archaeologists and culture historians as the reservoir from which the indigenous peoples and cultures of the Western Hemisphere must ultimately derive. Though Japan seems not to have been directly involved in this process, it is a fascinating study in itself: an almost laboratory situation for the study of cultural processes. For instance, Japan offers the oldest pottery in the world, antedating by thousands of years the presently known beginnings of ceramics anywhere else, and by a still longer time the beginnings of farming in the islands with which pottery has been traditionally associated the world over.

This book is intended for the nonspecialist: — the scholar in another field or interested general reader, — but should prove substantial enough for use as a textbook in East Asian archaeology or as supplementary reading in Old World prehistory. It is in consequence purposely not over-technical or detailed, and the emphasis is on the broader picture. I have sought to focus on long-term trends, overall patterns, and processes at work, as well as on cultural relationships and influences, human adaptation to the environments encountered, and ecological relationships to the surrounding natural world. In essence, it aims to be a work of interpretation rather than just a descriptive survey. In particular I have endeavored to avoid producing the usual catalogue of artifacts and have substituted illustrations rather than cluttering the text with minutiae. Selected chapter bibliographies will guide the reader who desires further detail and explanation; insofar as possible they are limited to works in English. The interested student is also urged to consult the relevant bibliographies and surveys of recent fieldwork that appeared periodically in the journal *Asian Perspectives* through volume 14.

Northeast Asia in Prehistory is a distillation of twenty years of research on the area. The data have been derived from critical study and analysis of Russian and Japanese language sources, from personal contact and correspondence with the leading Soviet and Japanese archaeologists in the field, from my own visits to and examination of collections in the U.S.S.R., Mongolia, and Japan, and from fieldwork and studies carried out by my former students and now colleagues in Japan, Korea, and Siberia.

Throughout, radiocarbon dates are cited in the form prescribed by the journal *Radiocarbon*. A list of the symbols identifying the laboratory responsible for each date (e.g., GaK, LE) may be consulted in the same publication. Dates specifically given in calendar years have been corrected in accordance with the correction tables published in *MASCA Newsletter* 9, no. 1 (August 1973).

For advice and critical comments on the draft manuscript I am greatly indebted to Tatsuo Kobayashi, Peter Bleed, L. L. Sample, and Roger Powers. In particular, chapter 5 is based primarily on studies carried out by Peter Bleed, to whom all credit should accrue. I wish to thank Sosuke Sugihara, Chosuke Serizawa, Richard K. Beardsley, and Atsuko Okada for kind permission to reproduce illustrations. Other acknowledgements will be found in the captions. Hiroaki Okada was very helpful in arranging for photographs of certain Japanese specimens.

CHESTER S. CHARD

Madison, Wisconsin

October 1973

Northeast Asia in Prehistory

1 Northeast Asia in the Pleistocene

The general tempo of Pleistocene studies in Siberia and Japan has increased considerably in recent years, marked by active field work and publication. These studies have embraced geology, palaeontology, and palynology as well as archaeology. As a result, we have at our disposal today a tremendously larger body of data than was available, say, twenty years ago.[1] Yet our overall picture is still unclear, confusing in many respects, and full of gaps. But when we consider how incomplete our knowledge of the European Pleistocene still remains despite intensive study of this small area for well over a hundred years, it should be no cause for wonder that Northeast Asia in the Pleistocene is not better understood. Moreover, we must expect that much present information will be subject to revision, especially in the case of Siberia — a vast area presenting many obstacles to study.

Our knowledge of adjoining regions is poor at best. Although extensive archaeological surveys carried out in Mongolia in the last few years have demonstrated abundant evidence of late Pleistocene human activity, very little of this has been reported to date; while our picture of the Pleistocene geology and ecology of Mongolia has scarcely advanced since the Andrews expeditions of the mid-1920s. Of Manchuria — very probably a key area for human history in Northeast Asia — we can only say that man seems to have been present in the Upper Pleistocene. Korea, also crucial because of its geographical position, has been a blank spot. The first evidence of Palaeolithic man in either North or South Korea has only just come to light.

The major lacunae hampering reconstruction of human history in Pleistocene Northeast Asia are the lack of skeletal material (or of any bone remains in Japan), the very small number of radiocarbon dates from archaeological

1. In fact, human presence in Japan during the Pleistocene was not documented until the first excavation of the Iwajuku site in 1949, despite extensive and intensive archaeological study of this small, accessible, and densely populated country dating back to 1879. Yet in the relatively short time since, some five hundred sites have come to light. This seemingly incongruous situation apparently stemmed from a general assumption on the part of archaeologists that no cultural remains were to be expected in the Pleistocene loam formations that underlie the humus levels in many parts of the country. Since these loams were considered to have been formed by volcanic ash deposition, there was a tendency to visualize Pleistocene Japan as a barren land unsuitable for human occupancy. It is a striking object lesson for the prehistorian.

sites (usually only single dates), and the difficulty in correlating local geological events and climatic phases with those elsewhere. There is also the scarcity of data, either archaeological or ecological, from key areas such as the Siberian Pacific coast and the far north, as well as Manchuria and Korea. Many current views and generalizations are inevitably based on negative evidence, involving the unlikely assumption that the picture as known today will remain relatively unchanged by future work.

There is no firmly dated and irreproachable evidence of human presence in Northeast Asia much before the final glaciation, although there are archaeological materials (especially in Mongolia) that must belong to earlier times, as well as finds in older geological contexts that are not universally accepted as human handiwork. These materials will be discussed presently. In the light of man's ability relatively early in the Middle Pleistocene to cope successfully with the rigorous environment of North China equipped only with what strikes us as a rather rudimentary technology, there would seem to be no reason why he should not have spread farther north and east unless hindered by geographic or climatic barriers. Rather than simply bowing to the negative evidence, let us rather see what would have been available to early man in Northeast Asia, and then, with what aid archaeology can supply, attempt to infer some picture of human history here in these earlier times — down to approximately 30,000 years ago.

Here, as elsewhere, Pleistocene man must be seen against the background of a changing world. Not only did the climatic fluctuations result in very different environments through time in a given area — some of which may as yet have been beyond his abilities, others of which doubtless inspired cultural adaptations — but fluctuating sea levels expanded or contracted coastal plain and littoral habitats and provided or denied access to offshore islands and continents. Glaciation itself, which because of inadequate precipitation was remarkably limited in this part of Eurasia, must have had little if any effect on the course of human history here.

The great boreal forest or taiga of Siberia was established in essentially its present character early in the Pleistocene and was never wholly displaced, although its extent fluctuated with climatic change. Even during the periods of maximum cold it persisted in the form of groves in a forest-steppe landscape. Central and southern Siberia constituted the major refugium for the forests of northern Eurasia at such times; elsewhere north of the arid zone, steppe and tundra stretched from Atlantic to Pacific. In contrast, the forests of Europe (the other great temperate forest area of the continent) were repeatedly obliterated and reconstituted; their present form is quite recent.

The taiga was an unattractive habitat for early man. Game was limited and scattered, and vegetable food virtually nonexistent. An effective adaptation was worked out very early in postglacial times, and subsequently the zone was extensively though sparsely occupied. But there is reason to feel that it may have been off limits to man in the Pleistocene and thus have constituted an effective barrier. The mixed forests of the Lower Amur-Maritime-Korea region of milder climate present a different situation. Due to lack of fossil remains we cannot assess the animal resources, but these forests are qualitatively not unlike those of interglacial Europe, which we know supported human populations. The northern half of the Japanese islands offered an approximately similar habitat, while the subtropical forests of the south must have been even more inviting. Many of the animals hunted by man in North China were also present in Japan.

The other types of habitat lying north and east of the known human world of Peking Man and his descendants are the forest steppe and the steppe. The forest steppe was optimal for game. The evidence suggests, not surprisingly, that it was the favored habitat of late glacial man in Siberia, and we may expect this to have been the case earlier as well. The drier true steppe offered less game and restricted the activity of primitive hunters to the vicinity of rivers and lakes, but there are indications that such localities were also the scene of early human activity.

During the Holstein interglacial, at the time of the later occupations of Choukoutien, the great bulk of Siberia was covered by taiga and thus must have lain outside the human world. Evidence suggests, however, a zone of forest steppe in southern Trans-Baikal and Manchuria, warm mixed forests in the Lower Amur-Maritime-Korea area, and steppe or desert conditions in Mongolia. Assuming ability to cope with the mixed forest at this time, all of these zones may have been occupied by *Homo erectus* populations, with this occupation in Mongolia limited to riverine localities. The Altai region was also half-surrounded by a belt of forest steppe to the west and north which included the middle Yenisei valley. This belt seems to have been linked on the south with the Mongolian steppe (and hence ultimately with North China) and also with Central Asia, where possibly early human tools have been discovered. A coastline essentially like the present is assumed, which would mean that the Japanese islands were isolated and probably still uninhabited.

The succeeding Riss cold period was the time of the maximum (Samarov) glaciation of Siberia, though this affected primarily the northwest and the mountain ranges of the northeast, and temperatures do not seem to have been as low as those of the late Pleistocene Würm glaciations. At the time of this maximum, steppe and desert-steppe conditions prevailed over southern Siberia, Trans-Baikal, Mongolia, Manchuria, and the Amur valley. This was basically the same environment that then characterized all of ice-free Europe, except such southern extremities as Portugal, Italy, and the Balkan coast. Populations of non-Acheulean tradition seem to have existed in central and eastern Europe under such conditions; the same should have been true in East

Table 1. Time Scale of Climatic Periods

Geologic Periods			Climatic Phases	Years B.P. (before present)	Siberia
Pleistocene	Lower		Mosbachian		
	Middle		Mindel		
			Holstein		
			Riss (Samarov)		
	Upper		Eemian (Kazantsev)		
			Early Würm (Zyrianka)	70-40,000 Yrs. 45,000 maximum	
			Aurignacian Oscillations (Karginsk)	40-30,000 Yrs.	
			Main Würm (Sartan)	First Half 30-21,000 Yrs.	
				Last Half 21-13,000 Yrs.	Siberian Palaeolithic
			Terminal Pleistocene	13-10,000 Yrs.	Siberian Palaeolithic
Holocene	Postglacial			9,000	Epipalaeolithic or Holocene Palaeolithic
				8,000	
			Post-Pleistocene climatic optimum	7,000	Early Neolithic (Aldan)
				6,000	
			3000 B.C.	5,000	Bel'kachinsk (Aldan)
			2000 B.C..	4,000	Late Neolithic (Aldan)
			1000 B.C.	3,000	
			0 A.D.	2,000	"Bronze Age"
			1000 A.D.	1,000	"Iron Age"
			1950 A.D.	Present	

Mongolia	Steppes	Korea	Japan
Initial settlement? (Musteroid)		Kul'po I?	Earliest sites?
"Upper Palaeolithic"		Kul'po II	"Preceramic"
"Upper Palaeolithic"			First pottery
			Initial Jomon
Epipalaeolithic		Early Neolithic	
		Chodo stage	
		Mokto stage	Early Jomon
		Pusan stage	
		Tudo stage	Middle Jomon
	Afanasievo Andronovo Karasuk		Late Jomon
Slab graves		"Bronze Age"	Final Jomon
Hsiung-Nü	Early Nomad	Iron	Yayoi
	Tashtyk Turks		Kofun

Asia. In a large area of central Siberia the taiga was reduced to forest steppe, and a similar fate befell the mixed forests of the Pacific coast, which survived intact only in Korea and doubtless Japan as well. This Pacific type of forest steppe, at least, was quite similar to the environment of the southern extremities of Europe at that time. The far northeast of Siberia, almost walled off by glaciated mountain ranges, was tundra. Thus most of Siberia during Riss times became optimum habitat for large game animals, and their presence is well documented. Steppe forms such as the saiga moved *north* now (not south, away from the periglacial conditions) and mingled with more typically arctic fauna. This was a time of extensive animal migration to Alaska, and beyond into continental North America when conditions allowed, including forms such as *Mammonteus trogontherii* which preferred warmer conditions. If the human populations of East Asia had achieved the necessary adaptation, Siberia would have been a happy hunting ground indeed; but in terms of overall human history this capability does not seem to appear until later.

The lowered sea levels of Riss times meant the establishment of land connections with southern Japan and between the Japanese islands, as evidenced by the presence of elements of the Middle Pleistocene fauna of North China throughout, remnants of which lingered on into the subsequent Eemian interglacial. Since these are the animals associated with Peking Man, and since the Yellow Sea for a time would have been a plain, doubtless populated, it is hard to believe that Japan was not first settled during this period. The exposed arctic continental shelf and Bering Platform provided the bulk of the tundra zone. The low water also would have exposed a shelf along the coast of the Sea of Okhotsk providing access from the Amur region to Kamchatka, the Anadyr valley, and Alaska — access impossible by this route with the normal sea levels during interglacial or postglacial times, owing to rugged terrain. The road to the New World was open, but man was probably not yet ready to use it. At the same time, access westward to Europe was virtually blocked, at least during the Riss maximum, by the glaciers of the Russian plain, which closely approached the expanded Caspian Sea.

Environmental and geographical conditions essentially similar to those of the Holstein interglacial returned with the warm climate of the Eemian (Kazantsev in Siberian terminology). Siberia once more became unfavorable for man except in the forest-steppe zone of the south, the steppes of Mongolia-Manchuria, and the mixed forests of the Far East. Game must have been concentrated especially in the former. Access to the New World was cut off, but tectonic instability in the region of Japan may have counteracted rising sea levels. Some geologists believe that southern Japan was linked to Korea during at least part of the Eemian, although the northern half experienced inundation of lowlands by sea levels substantially higher than the present to the extent that Hokkaido was reduced to two small islands by the flooding of the intervening Ishikari plain. Any human populations in Japan during the Eemian may therefore not have been as isolated as has generally been assumed.

Eventually, beginning probably around 70,000 years ago, deteriorating climate brought on the Early Würm glaciation (Zyrianka in Siberia) which seems to have reached its peak approximately 45,000 years ago. Although temperatures were more severe than during the earlier Riss (Samarov), the ice was considerably less extensive. Sea level dropped sufficiently to restore access to the New World and to the island of Hokkaido (virtually an appendage of Siberia at such times). That southern Japan was at some point connected with Korea or the Yellow Sea area is indicated by the arrival now of a new fauna from the loess region of North China. More open conditions returned to Siberia, game animals proliferated and ranged widely once more. Since periglacial Europe was exploited successfully at this time by Neanderthal man, we may suppose that the contemporary East Asian Neanderthaloid populations had an equal potential unless some significant technological differential existed. Contact with the Near East and the Russian plain (which was first settled by the beginning of this period) was possible by way of Central Asia.

Following the cold peak, the climate warmed rapidly, and some time after 40,000 years ago northern Eurasia was in an interstadial (Karginsk) with forests restored and land connections severed by rising sea levels. Human populations by now were entirely of modern type.

Having surveyed the potentials for human existence in Northeast Asia down to about 30,000 years ago, let us turn to the actual remains of human activity that may reflect this earlier time. (Remains of man himself are totally lacking.) Contiguous areas are no less important, both for indirect evidence and as possible sources of cultural influence and of people themselves. They will be considered first.

The closest Europeans were those on the South Russian Plain, which was not settled until late in the Eemian at the earliest, with the settlers stemming both from the Caucasus and East-Central Europe. In still earlier times this steppe environment seems to have been uninviting or unfeasible for adjacent populations despite its undoubted game resources — a phenomenon that may have relevance for similar situations in East Asia. The cultural traditions established here were of Mousteroid type through the Early Würm (exemplified by such sites as Volgograd) and later, in the subsequent warm interstadial, developed into plains-adapted hunting cultures using projectile weapons equipped with bifacial stone points (e.g., Kostenki).

Central Asia was settled from the Middle East by peoples of Neanderthaloid type (e.g., Teshik-Tash) at about the same time, and as part of the same general expansion of human populations beyond previous frontiers. This settlement, however, was confined to the highland areas of the south and east, or their immediate vicinity, and is not known to have extended to the steppes. The steppe adaptation seems to have developed on the plains of eastern Europe, while the Middle Eastern populations were ecologically adapted to a highland-foothill habitat and doubtless a more generalized economy. Their technological tradition is commonly labeled Levallois-Mousterian. It was conservative, retained archaic-looking features, and did not develop projectile weapons and bifacial stone-working technique. Continued northward movement in Central Asia through highland zones of similar habitat would have brought these people eventually to the Altai region and thence into Mongolia, without necessitating any changes in economy, technology, or ecological patterns.

This settlement of Central Asia by Middle Eastern Neanderthaloid populations was not necessarily the first human occupation of the area. The same highland portion has also yielded a number of localities with surface assemblages of very crude tools that have been likened to the Soan of the Punjab or the pebble tool industries of East Asia. Unfortunately, it is impossible to date these, and the known occurrence of very late survivals of crude technology in this same region makes typological dating unconvincing. However, the possibility cannot be ruled out that at some past time the western margin of the East Asian chopper/chopping tool tradition extended as far as the highlands of Central Asia.

In eastern Asia, the contiguous area is north China, which establishes that man of *Homo erectus* type was close to Northeast Asia as early as the Middle Pleistocene, and was capable of coping with quite rigorous conditions. But there are only suggestions of direct relationship between Chinese cultures and anything to the north or east prior to the late Pleistocene. In this category are a few recent finds in Korea and Japan which will be noted presently.

A demonstration that man had entered the New World at the time of the Early Würm land connection would of course establish his presence in extreme northeastern Siberia at least by the final stages of that period, regardless of the absence of Siberian evidence. Sufficient data are now at hand to show beyond any doubt that the New World had been settled prior to the creation of the final Würm/Wisconsin ice barrier which blocked all further ingress from Alaska until postglacial times. The time of closure of this barrier is uncertain, and prior availability of the Bering Land Bridge would be required to permit direct migration. At least one geological authority on the subject feels that man would need to have been in Alaska prior to 32,000 years ago, which would seem to involve crossing from Siberia at least before the end of the Early Würm/Zyrianka. Some also see evidence — admittedly inconclusive — of a non-projectile-point tradition of crude heavy tools in the New World

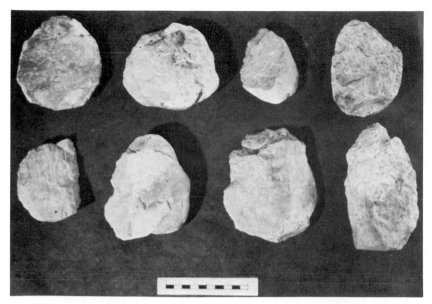

Figure 1.1. Artifacts from Ulalinka Creek (photograph by Roger Powers).

whose closest analogs would appear to lie in the Eemian Tingts'un industry of North China. Should this possibility be substantiated, it would suggest passage through Siberia in Early Würm/Zyrianka times. The route was open and feasible; only the proof is lacking.

Turning to the archaeological record in Northeast Asia itself, there are suggestions of early human presence at three points scattered across southern Siberia: (1) Ulalinka Creek at Gornoaltaisk (Altai region), where what are described as crude artifacts were found in an apparently old geological deposit far beneath a level of typical Upper Palaeolithic material (fig. 1.1); (2) Malyi Kot (Kuda River valley near Irkutsk), where a tooth of *Mammonteus trogontherii* and a chopper were found in the dirt from an excavation, but without proof of association or evidence of the original context; and (3) Filomoshki on the Zeia River (a tributary of the Middle Amur), where possible artifacts were found in basal gravels suggesting considerable antiquity.[2] At best these finds suggest that we may ultimately hope that better and more precisely dated evidence of early man in Siberia will come to light.

The largest body of possibly early material in Northeast Asia has been discovered in recent years in Mongolia through the extensive work of the Soviet-Mongolian expeditions directed by A. P. Okladnikov. Little has yet

2. Somewhat to the west of our area an indubitable flake blade with faceted platform was recently recovered from a deposit near Rubtsovsk, ascribed by geologists to the Riss glaciation.

been reported of this mass of data, and local conditions pose major problems in interpretation. The sites regarded as early are all on the surface, and temporal placement is dependent on such shaky bases as typology, weathering, and patination. Generally speaking, the sites are located in arid regions and must represent periods when the climate was considerably wetter than it is today. Such pluvial conditions are conventionally correlated with glacial episodes on a worldwide basis. The geologist Ravskii, however, believed that pluvial periods in Mongolia correspond to the more humid phases of interglacials and perhaps the early stages of ensuing glaciations. In his view the present semi-desert areas were colder and drier during glacial maxima, with loess being removed. Lake basins were filled, but with melt water from mountain glaciers, not by rainfall. If this hypothesis is correct, we could infer that Palaeolithic sites not associated with former lakes or major rivers must date from some point in interglacial or interstadial periods or to the beginning of glaciations; those associated with lake beds or rivers could also have been occupied toward the end of glaciations when melting was in progress; while during glacial maxima the area was perhaps too dry for human use, which would have impelled movement elsewhere — for instance, to Siberia. However, such a reconstruction is still problematical.

Sites in Mongolia regarded as early are characterized by prepared-platform cores and flakes, discoidal cores, and "Mousterian" flakes, as well as flakes with plain platform. There are also occasional pebble tools, but no handaxes. Very similar assemblages are widespread in Soviet Central Asia and the Near East, where the term "Levalloiso-Mousterian" is applied to them by Soviet writers. There is no reason to doubt that these Mongolian sites represent an intrusion from the western world, and perhaps the initial human settlement of Mongolia.

The Soviet investigators, Okladnikov and Larichev, believe it possible to assign a number of these early surface assemblages to three chronological stages on a typological basis. The oldest of these, represented by the workshop site near Bogdo-Somon, is considered to reflect archaic techniques of stone working corresponding to late Acheulean or early Mousterian levels of technology in the west. The second stage is characterized particularly by the Levallois technique; such assemblages were found at Ottson-Man't on the Chinese frontier; at Ikh-Bogdo in the southwestern Gobi, where there is no trace of former water; and also by the Hungarian archaeologist Gabori near Mandal-Gobi. Other assemblages near Bogdo-Somon and Ottson-Man't that are regarded as more "classical Mousterian" in appearance are placed in the third stage. Belonging to the same general time level as these early sites is the initial use of the huge Arts-Bogdo quarry-workshop in the southwestern part of the central Gobi — although its major use was in the "Upper Palaeolithic" and in later times as well, down to the Neolithic.[3] This site complex covers an area of over one hundred square kilometers, with concentrations in places of up to three hundred artifacts per square meter. In sheer quantity of material and duration of use this complex probably could not be duplicated anywhere else in the world. When more adequately studied it should shed much light on techniques and manufacturing processes, as well as on diffusion in prehistoric times, since the products apparently spread far and wide, at least in later periods.

All these early-seeming materials reflecting pluvial conditions in present arid regions might be correlated with the onset of the Early Würm/Zyrianka glaciation if Ravskii's hypothesis is correct. On cultural-historical grounds it seems impossible to consider them any earlier; but they might well be later. Any dating at present is tentative.

In Japan, as in Siberia, there are only a handful of possibly early sites as compared with the large number dating from the final Würm stage. In this category are Fujiyama, Yamaderayama, Gongenyama, and Hoshino in the northern Kanto region, and Sozudai, Nyu, and Fukui Cave (level xv) in Kyushu. The first two are Early Würm deposits that yielded a few massive stone specimens believed by some to be artifacts. The two small collections of flakes and crude implements from Gongenyama are unquestionably man-made, but their provenience must remain in question. They are believed to have come from late Early Würm deposits, but unfortunately the geological interpretation was made at a later date and had to be based on a profile some fifty meters away from the actual site which by then had been completely destroyed. The three lowest cultural levels at Hoshino are well dated to the Early Würm, though their precise placement within it is in dispute. The sizable lithic inventory is said to be characterized technologically by the detaching of flakes from prepared cores — a technique comparable to but not necessarily related to the Levallois of the west. Its closest affinities would seem to lie in the Fenho valley of North China (Tingts'un). There is also some trace of flat bifacial retouch. The first materials recovered from the site were not universally accepted as artifacts, but subsequent finds have greatly strengthened the case.[4]

3. There is an apparent scarcity of suitable lithic raw material for technological purposes in much of Mongolia. Main dependence was on jasper, sources of which are concentrated in certain localities. These restricted sources seem to have been exploited by the population of a large area over long periods of time, or until exhausted. Quarry and workshop sites in Mongolia are thus major foci of human activity that reflect long spans of human history in a given area. They also suggest the necessity for a certain mobility in the patterns of life.

4. 1970–71 re-excavation of the famous Iwajuku site in northern Kanto by Chosuke Serizawa has revealed a deeply buried horizon of uncertain age but certainly older than 30,000 years. Some of the artifacts are said to be reminiscent of Choukoutien.

In Kyushu a large collection of quartzite specimens was excavated from what is believed to be an Early Würm deposit at Sozudai. The dating, however, depends on very tenuous long-range correlations, and a number of scholars are reluctant to accept the specimens as man-made. Fifty artifacts, half of them properly archaic-looking choppers and chopping tools, were found at Nyu, but their exact provenience is uncertain and the early geological dating of the supposed deposit is controversial. (It has been pointed out that equally crude implements of this sort occur in Holocene Jomon assemblages.) The early age of level xv at Fukui Cave is based solely on a radiocarbon date of greater than 31,900 years, and while such single dates are generally not accepted as conclusive, it is not inconsistent with the stratigraphy and dating of the rest of this important site. The assemblage of large bifaces, points, and large blade-like flakes, however, would not otherwise have been attributed to such an early period. The verdict on this case must remain open.[5]

Certain inferences or hypotheses as to human history in Northeast Asia prior to approximately 30,000 years ago might be drawn from the body of environmental and archaeological data surveyed above. Siberia during glacial periods would appear to have offered resources and conditions equal or superior to those of contemporary glacial Europe, which held at least some populations at these times. On the other hand, the reverse may have been true during warm interglacials when the inhospitable taiga covered most of the area and man may have withdrawn to the forest steppes along the southern edge and the mixed forests of the Far East. The initial settlement of Japan may have occurred from North China during the low sea levels of the Riss glaciation, though there is no direct evidence, and subsequent opportunities seem also to have been available during the Eemian interglacial and the Early Würm cold period.

There are traces suggesting an early pebble tool occupation of southern Siberia — evidently in the zone of forest steppe. It could thus have occurred at any time and would not necessarily have led to further movement northward. It is tempting to correlate this with the possible early pebble tool expansion into Central Asia. In both cases the populations would seem to have withdrawn subsequently. Later occupations came from outside the areas.

What seems at present to have been the initial settlement of Mongolia took place from the west by Central Asian groups of Levallois-Mousterian technical traditions, perhaps in the early stages of the Zyrianka (Early Würm) cold

5. 1968 excavations in Yamashita-cho Cave in the vicinity of Naha, Okinawa, revealed human bones underlying a level radiocarbon-dated at 32,100 years ago. Still more recent investigations on Okinawa at the Minatogawa limestone quarry are reported to have yielded remains of a number of individuals, along with deer and boar bones and a radiocarbon date of 18,300 years. No cultural remains seem to have been associated in either case. Such preservation of bone, a rare exception in the Japanese islands, is due to the limestone context.

period. It could scarcely have been earlier; it might have been considerably later. This movement does not seem at present to have proceeded the short remaining distance into southern Siberia. The lack of a still earlier pebble tool occupation of Mongolia is puzzling.

The possibility cannot be dismissed of a move during early Zyrianka times from the general North China area to the New World. This would probably have involved a population of general Neanderthaloid type. Most New World scholars peremptorily reject this possibility on the grounds that no human remains of this type occur in the New World. The similar lack of early *Homo sapiens sapiens* remains for some reason does not seem to be equal evidence against the settlement of the Americas by modern man. At least one leading physical anthropologist, W. S. Laughlin, sees nothing improbable about the possible former presence of Neanderthaloid forms in the New World.

Another possibility, toward the very end of Zyrianka times, is the movement of plains-adapted hunters across Siberia from the South Russian Plain and into Alaska. Such a movement has been postulated for early in the final Würm glaciation, but depending on the time of closure of the Canadian ice barrier, this earlier crossing to Alaska may seem probable.

Turning now to the late Pleistocene — the cold period that witnessed the onset, peak, and decline of the main or final Würm glaciation (called Sartan in Siberia) — Northeast Asia presented a more hospitable appearance than did Europe at that time. North of the Pyrenees, Alps, and Balkans, Europe was primarily covered with tundra and loess steppe. Extensive areas underwent glaciation. Siberia east of the Yenisei, on the other hand, was mostly forest steppe, with tundra in the northeast (much of it on emerged continental shelf). Glaciation was minimal, confined to the northwest corner and scattered mountain glaciers elsewhere which interposed no barriers. There were small patches of loess steppe in the south (upper Angara valley, middle Yenisei, Altai-Sayan foothills), never far from trees, that seem to have been especially favored by man. However, we know that he was also present in the forest steppe at 63 degrees north latitude — far to the north of any human occupation in western Europe — and also on the tundra of Kamchatka. Mongolia and Manchuria were loess steppe and desert; Korea and southern Japan were covered with mixed forests. Hokkaido formed part of Siberia and was environmentally rather similar. The main and southern islands of Japan constituted a single land mass that was very briefly linked with Hokkaido at one end and perhaps with Korea at the other. It is known that much of the Yellow Sea floor was exposed at the lowest sea level (about 18,000 years ago), but current opinion is that the Korean Strait remained in being, although reduced to a width of 10 kilometers. Some animals evidently crossed, however, and it was probably by now no barrier to man. (The first settlers of Australia negotiated a more impressive water barrier at this general time.) Access from Siberia to the

Map 1.   Northeast Asia during the last glaciation. (Vegetation zones after Frenzel, 1968.)

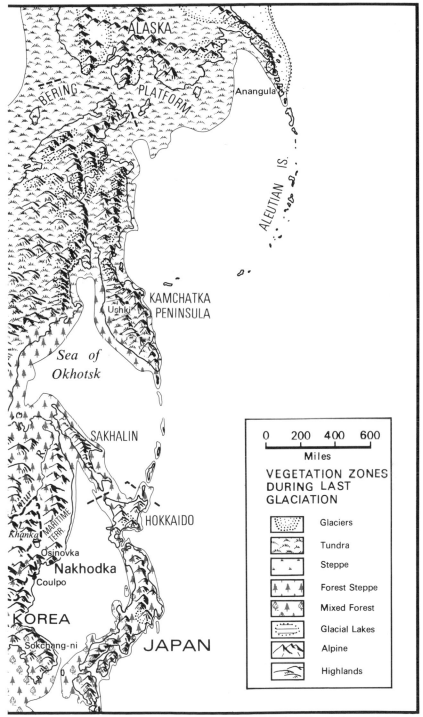

ALASKA

BERING PLATFORM

Anangula

ALEUTIAN IS.

Attu

KAMCHATKA
PENINSULA

Ushki

Sea of
Okhotsk

SAKHALIN

HOKKAIDO

Amur R.

MARITIME
TERR.

Khanka

Osinovka

Nakhodka

Coulpo

KOREA

Sokchang-ni

JAPAN

| 0 | 200 | 400 | 600 |

Miles

VEGETATION ZONES
DURING LAST
GLACIATION

Glaciers

Tundra

Steppe

Forest Steppe

Mixed Forest

Glacial Lakes

Alpine

Highlands

University of Wisconsin Cartographic Laboratory

New World was easy (the Bering land bridge attained a north-south width of 1300 miles), and animals roamed freely. The unglaciated portions of Alaska were teeming with game, and Siberia must have presented a similar picture. Indeed, the Alaskan climate at the peak of glaciation has been described as no worse than that of its north slope today.

With the few tentative exceptions noted previously, all Pleistocene archaeological materials from Siberia fall within this late glacial period. (The Ust'-Kanskaia Cave in the Altai, initially placed in the Karginsk warm interstadial, is now considered undated, since both its fauna and tool types persisted into later times.) Since there is no evidence at present of immediately preceding occupation — in particular, no reflection of the extensive Levallois-Mousterian presence in neighboring Mongolia — it is assumed that the late Pleistocene cultures of Siberia (the "Siberian Palaeolithic") all represent intrusions from outside. The most obvious possible source would seem to be that lying closest, so let us first examine the situation in Mongolia.

In contrast to the putative early sites which are concentrated in arid regions, the so-called "Upper Palaeolithic" occupation of Mongolia was generally in the proximity of major rivers and thus could have existed under present climatic conditions or even under drier and colder ones. These later sites also represent a very different technological tradition, with continuity limited primarily to survival of the Levallois technique. They are characterized especially by the abundance of pebble tools: choppers and chopping tools in particular, gigantic skreblos,[6] axe-like implements made of river cobbles, and distinctive cores. The source for such a tradition must lie in China. This technological break has suggested a temporal hiatus as well, and it has been hypothesized by Soviet scholars that the earlier population moved out of Mongolia entirely when the country turned to desert — perhaps during the first cold maximum following the Eemian — to be replaced at a later time by very different groups pressing northward out of eastern Asia. Since these apparently later "Upper Palaeolithic" sites are situated in areas that could have been occupied under a wider range of climatic conditions, it is difficult to place them in time. However, inasmuch as they represent the same tradition found in much of the Siberian Palaeolithic, they probably cover a comparable span of time from roughly 20,000 to perhaps 7000 years ago, with the exception of the lowest level at the following site.

The development of "Upper Palaeolithic" culture in Mongolia is considered to be reflected in the sequence at the stratified Moil'tyn-am site located across the Orkhon River from Karakorum. The lowest of the four levels contained a blend of Levallois-Mousterian (i.e., Levallois cores, discoidal cores, Mousterian-type points) and East Asian choppers, chopping tools, and

6. A sort of massive side scraper, very typical of the Siberian Palaeolithic (see fig. 1.19).

skreblos, associated with a yellow loam stratum. A possible correlation of the latter with the Malan loess of North China has been suggested, but this will have to await further study of the geology of the site. In view of the mixed nature of the assemblage, giving the impression of being transitional between the earlier and later sites, the suggestion is not improbable. Such a transitional industry would, however, seem to belie any hypothesis of the abandonment of Mongolia by its former population, followed, after a hiatus, by a totally new population. Certainly the desert areas were abandoned, but the earlier people may have hung on in the less arid northern half of the country, to mix subsequently with the newcomers from the south, as the lowest level at Moil'tyn-am might suggest.

The second and third horizons from the bottom seem to be treated together and equated with the typical Siberian Palaeolithic. In addition to the strong pebble tool element, there is an efflorescence of various forms of scrapers and the appearance of a true blade technique with prismatic cores which the Soviet investigators believe to represent a local development out of the earlier Levallois prepared cores and flake-blades — an independent invention, or evolution, out of a widespread early technological tradition which might therefore be expected to ensue in other parts of the Old World as well.[7]

A very large number of sites have now been discovered in the northern two-thirds of Mongolia (i.e., north of the true desert) which seem to be generally equated by their discoverers with levels II and III at Moil'tyn-am and which therefore indicate the widespread and relatively intensive human occupation of the country at this time (terminal Pleistocene).

Late Pleistocene Siberia is very clearly divisible into two primary culture areas, reflecting essentially different environmental conditions: one is the Far East (Amur-Maritime) area of milder climate and mixed forests; the other, all of interior and northeast Siberia, characterized by a more rigorous, continental-type climate and predominantly taiga or tundra habitat. (In both areas the respective forest types dwindled to forest steppe at the glacial maximum.) The fauna differed as much as the vegetation (for example, the tiger is diagnostic of the Far East). It is scarcely surprising that the contrasting resources and ecology should be represented by distinctive cultural features.

Pleistocene remains in the Far East have only recently come to light; they are still scanty and little known. When people speak of the "Siberian Palaeolithic" it is the interior culture area that is meant. The latter has been

7. A typical blade-and-burin industry of European Aurignacoid type occurs only at Altan-Bulaq on the northern frontier of present-day Mongolia. Burins are very rare in Mongolia, suggesting the absence also of bone technology, a prime Aurignacoid diagnostic, otherwise difficult to determine owing to the general nonpreservation of bone remains. It is thus curious that there seems to be a definite Aurignacoid element in the mixed complex at Shuitungkou in the Ordos region to the south, securely dated by the associated late Pleistocene fauna.

known since the first finds by Savenkov on the Yenisei in 1884, and there has been a natural tendency to characterize the "Siberian Palaeolithic" in terms of the diagnostic traits at the famous Afontova Gora site there. Its peculiar features as contrasted with the Palaeolithic of all other then known regions promoted an initial tendency, still prevalent today, to view the "Siberian Palaeolithic" as a single and rather monolithic entity. In postwar years, as the body of available evidence increased, it became evident that this concept was not applicable to all sites and was true only in very general terms. Recent discoveries make it increasingly evident that we must distinguish not only discrete regional manifestations but differences through time as well. And even the monolithic viewpoint has stressed the complex and multiple origins of the tradition.

To account for the manifestations of the interior Palaeolithic discovered to date, at least four different sources must be invoked: (1) the early plains-adapted hunters of southern Russia with their bifacial stone points; (2) the later Aurignacoid plains hunters of the same region with their unifacial blade and burin industry and emphasis on bone technology; (3) the Levallois-Mousterian tradition of Central Asia; and (4) the heavy-tool pebble technology of Mongolia which must have deep roots in eastern Asia. No examples of "pure" components of any of these are known in Siberia itself, but since these roots are discrete areally or temporally, mixture most likely occurred after arrival there.

Bifacial stone points are extremely rare: they are found in only two sites of glacial age — Diuktai Cave in Yakutia and the Military Hospital site in Irkutsk. The most conspicuous Aurignacoid manifestation occurs at the famous site of Mal'ta with its semi-subterranean dwellings and rich bone art, but already mixed with Central Asian elements. The Levallois-Mousterian technical tradition is most strongly represented in the Altai region (Ust'-Kanskaia, etc.), though evident elsewhere. Most widespread of all is the use of heavy tools made from river cobbles (pebbles), especially the large side scraper (skreblo) whcih many consider the index fossil of the Siberian Palaeolithic.

Since the dating of most interior Siberian sites within the last glacial is still uncertain, imprecise, or controversial, their temporal relationships must be held in abeyance. A chronological description of cultural history such as will be found in most standard accounts is thus not yet feasible, and it seems better to present the data at the moment in terms of regional manifestations.

The Mal'ta culture has been the most conspicuous in its distinctive features and spectacular finds. The Mal'ta site near Irkutsk has been excavated over an extent of six hundred square meters, revealing numerous dwellings (not necessarily all occupied simultaneously). Most of these are semi-subterranean, and utilized large animal bones to support a roof which incorporated a layer of interlaced reindeer antlers. These dwellings contain abundant remains of

Figure 1.2. Mal'ta: house 5 after removal of roof debris (after Gerasimov).

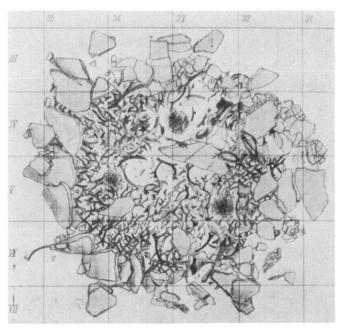

Figure 1.3. Mal'ta: house 5 as seen from above before removal of roof debris (after Gerasimov). (See also fig. 1.2.)

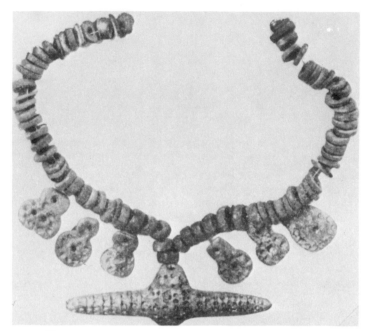

Figure 1.4. Mal'ta: necklace from child burial (after Abramova).

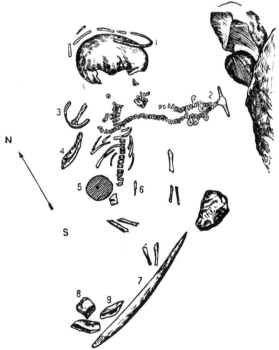

Figure 1.5. Mal'ta: child burial with necklace and other accompanying artifacts (after Gerasimov). (See also fig. 1.4.).

Figure 1.6. Mal'ta: carving of mammoth (after Gerasimov).

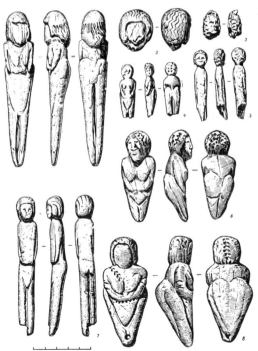

Figure 1.7. Mal'ta: female figurines (after Abramova).

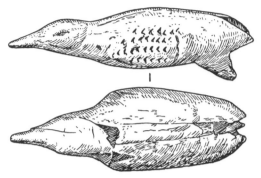

Figure 1.8. Mal'ta: carving of a loon (after Abramova).

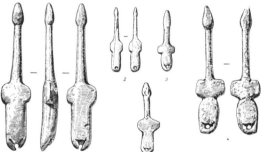

Figure 1.9. Mal'ta: schematic figures of waterfowl (after Abramova).

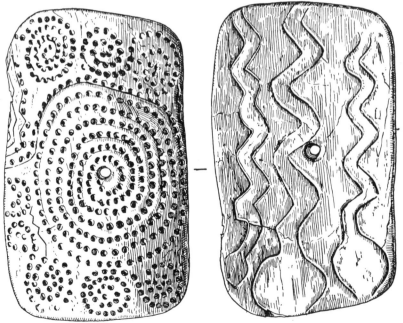

Figure 1.10. Mal'ta: carved plaque (after Abramova). (See also fig. 1.6.)

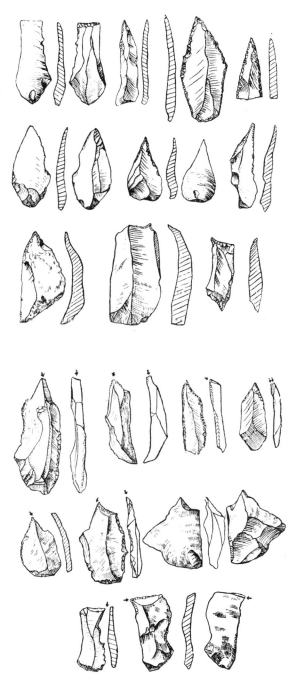

Figure 1.11. Mal'ta: pointed blade tools (above) and burins (below) (after Gerasimov). (See also fig. 1.12.)

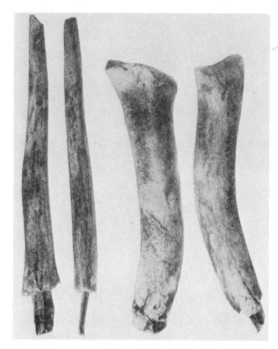

Figure 1.12. Mal'ta: stone cutting tools in antler handles (after Gerasimov).

domestic life, and the excavator, M. M. Gerasimov, discerns a clear division of the interior between men's and women's activities. Intellectual life is reflected in a child burial, in intentional burials of foxes after they had been skinned, and especially in the bone and ivory carvings, including female figurines. The economy was based on hunting the big game of the surrounding loess steppe — primarily mammoth, rhinoceros, and reindeer. Most tools were made from medium-sized prismatic blades of irregular shape taken from flint nodules. All this indicates a group tracing its origin to the South Russian Plain (Aurignacoid tradition), but one which had already absorbed a number of Siberian traits, mostly of ultimate Central Asian origin. A complex of the latter type is represented in the Achinsk site west of Krasnoyarsk, also of last glacial age, which is said to closely resemble the lithic inventory from Samarkand and other points in Soviet Central Asia as well as the non-Aurignacoid element at Mal'ta. Mal'ta in addition has some pebble choppers, but lacks the typical skreblos so common in Siberian Palaeolithic sites, and also such other frequent traits as pebble cores, wedge-shaped cores, microblades, or composite tools. These negative features, as well as an art style duplicated only at the nearby site of Buret', make the Mal'ta culture unique in Siberia. Its time placement is a matter of some interest. From the beginning, it has been *assumed* (for no particularly convincing reason) to represent the oldest stage of the Siberian Palaeolithic and thus to antedate all the other sites, and the evidence has been consistently interpreted accordingly, perhaps for no other reason. Actually, on the basis of geological, climatic, faunal, and cultural data, it could be placed almost anywhere in the final glaciation, and some geologists have argued for the preceding Karginsk interstadial or even the earlier Zyrianka glaciation, although neither would be consistent with the cultural picture. The most acceptable guess dates have been on the order of 15,000–18,000 years. Recently a radiocarbon date on fossil bone of 14,750±120 B.P. (GIN–97) has been announced. This will doubtless upset Soviet archaeologists; a single C14 age determination can of course always be questioned, and dates on bone can involve large errors, but it may well prove to be correct.

The uniqueness of the Mal'tá culture is further emphasized by the presence in the same general upper Angara valley area in late glacial times of two other dissimilar and unrelated complexes. One is represented at the Irkutsk Military Hospital site, the materials from which were lost many years ago. With only brief accounts remaining, our understanding of this potentially important site is badly handicapped. A conspicuous feature was the decorative bone art, unrelated to that at Mal'ta and described as much simpler and not realistic. Of particular interest were the bifacial foliate points, a possible survivor, as mentioned, of the pre-Aurignacoid technology practised by the earliest hunters of the south Russian Plain. Pebble choppers were also present. The other complex appears in the lower levels at Krasnyi IAr, now flooded by the Bratsk reservoir, where rhinoceros is associated with wedge-shaped cores, microblades, transverse burins, knives on large prismatic blades, ostrich egg-shell beads, skreblos, and choppers. This complex may be intrusive from Trans-Baikal, where some of the features are more common. The later levels at Krasnyi IAr are rather different.

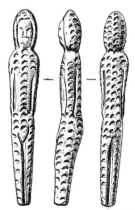

Figure 1.13. Buret': figurine showing possible fur clothing (after Abramova).

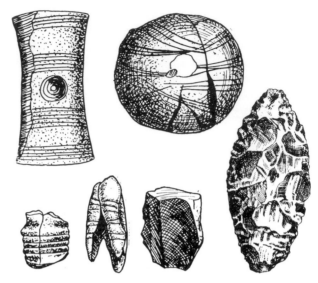

Figure 1.14. Artifacts from the Irkutsk Military Hospital site (after Larichev).

The Trans-Baikal sites such as Ikaral and Sannyi Mys (lower level) which contain a late glacial fauna (mammoth and rhinoceros) are characterized, like Mal'ta, by absence of the large Siberian skreblo and other heavy tools. Instead, they feature microblades from wedge-shaped or prismatic cores. Later horizons in this area are typically Siberian.

The other late Pleistocene sites of interior Siberia are by and large characterized by the use of pebbles as raw material, a really distinctive feature which sets Siberia and Mongolia rather sharply apart from contemporary Europe or the Africa-Mediterranean area. The skreblo is the commonest artifact type.

The famous Yenisei Palaeolithic sites with one exception seem to fall in the last half of the Sartan (final Würm) glaciation and can be associated with the sequence of terrace deposits of the Yenisei River and thus placed in relative order. Radiocarbon dates are also now available for several, although we can only assume that the samples dated came from the main cultural level of the particular site. The exception is the largest and probably most important site of all, Afontova Gora II, which is in a very different stratigraphic situation, making its geological placement subject to dispute. A new radiocarbon date of 20,900±300 (GIN–117) tends to agree with the latest geological interpretation, but creates a disturbing time gap of five to eight thousand years with respect to other sites which are culturally rather similar and should not be too far removed in time. Again, a single C14 date is not conclusive, and we do not know the precise position of the sample.

Over fifty other Palaeolithic sites have been found so far on the middle

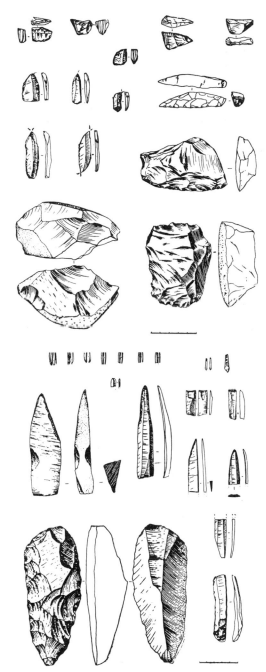

Figure 1.15. Krasnyi IAr: artifacts from the lower levels (after Medvedev).

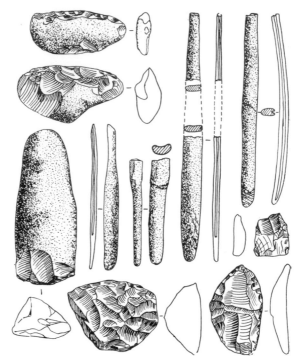

Figure 1.16. Artifacts from Afontova Gora II. Upper left, skreblos; upper right, slotted bone points (after Larichev).

Yenisei. The oldest firmly dated group, associated with the upper part of the alluvial sediments of the second terrace, includes Kipernyi Log (Kokorevo IV), with dates of 15,460±320 (LE–540) and 14,320±330 (LE–469); Telezhnyi Log (Kokorevo II), with a date of 13,330±100 (GIN–90); and Zabochka (Kokorevo I), with dates of 14,450±150 (LE–628), 13,330±50 (GIN–91), and 12,940±270 (LE–526) from different levels. A younger group, associated with the alluvium of the first terrace and considered to be post-Alleröd in European terms, includes Pereselencheskii Punkt and Biriusa.

The large and rich Afontova Gora II site (excavated in 1923–25) contains the only semi-subterranean dwellings in the Yenisei area. Several were found, but have not been as well studied as those at Mal'ta. One is described as an irregular oval 10 × 5–6 meters in size and 1.5–1.75 meters deep. The inhabitants of the site burned willow and larch for fuel and subsisted primarily on mammoth, reindeer, hare, ptarmigan, and arctic fox. Also occasionally hunted were saiga antelope, bison, horse, and cave lion. All investigators have recovered remains identified as dog or perhaps domesticated wolf. Among the refuse in one house were several human bones, suggesting the possibility of cannibalism.

With one possible exception, evidence of habitations at the other Yenisei sites is confined to characteristic slab-lined hearths presumably associated with some sort of impermanent above-ground structure. This shift in house type at what are presumed to be later sites is commonly explained as the result of climatic changes at the end of the last glaciation. However, a number of these sites show evidence of conditions just as cold as those prevailing at Afontova Gora and on cultural grounds, as noted, they should not be too widely separated in time. As an example of the other older Yenisei sites we may take Zabochka (Kokorevo I), of which eight hundred square meters have been excavated. It represents repeated seasonal camps of the same or culturally uniform groups. The inhabitants burned willow, birch, pine, and larch or fir in their slab-lined hearths, showing that at least groves of trees were present in the area in late glacial times. They hunted chiefly reindeer and hare, with an occasional horse, mountain sheep, aurochs, or bison. Of particular interest is a scapula of the latter pierced through with the antler point of a throwing spear (fig. 1.18).

There are no essential differences in the lithic inventory of these numerous sites of different ages which are scattered over a considerable distance from Krasnoyarsk to the Minusinsk Basin, although proportions and emphasis may differ. The large skreblos are the commonest tools; most others are made from blades removed from cores made of river pebbles, but there are some small tools from flint nodules. Bifacial chopping tools occur everywhere, but in small numbers. Wedge-shaped cores (core-scrapers) are typical in many

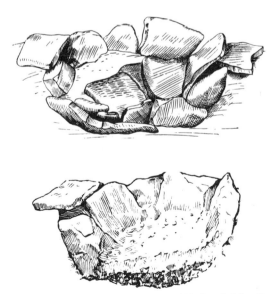

Figure 1.17. Zabochka: typical Yenisei Palaeolithic hearth (after Sosnovskii).

Figure 1.18. Zabochka (Kokorevo ɪ): bilaterally grooved bone point with inset stone blades piercing scapula of *Bison priscus* (photograph by Roger Powers).

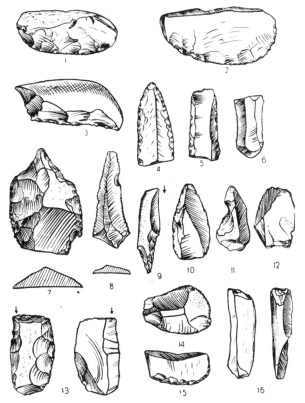

Figure 1.19. Stone tools from Zabochka. Numbers 1 and 2 are skreblos (after Sosnovskii).

cases. Stone points are rare except at Kokorevo I, and the same is true of burins — a strange situation in view of the wide use of bone and antler on the Yenisei. Slotted bone spear points, daggers, and knives with inserted stone blades are characteristic. Also present are "batons de commandment" (testifying to the intrusion or persistence of some Western elements), needles with eyes, picks, plain spear points, and ornaments such as perforated teeth, beads, and pendants. There is a striking absence of anything that could be called works of art.

The Yenisei Palaeolithic as a whole represents a very distinctive cultural tradition, and its initial stage has no analogies elsewhere as such, although individual traits can be matched. Its basic features can be seen persisting into later times, here and elsewhere, outlasting the Pleistocene. For instance, the same general cultural pattern with the typical skreblo and other heavy stone implements along with composite tools prevailed at the very beginning of the Holocene in Trans-Baikal (Oshurkovo) and the upper Angara valley (Verkholenskaia Gora). The latter, one of the famous sites of Siberia and long regarded as the type site for the latest stage of the Palaeolithic, was actually very inadequately known and has only recently been extensively restudied. The lowest of the three horizons here has been dated by radiocarbon to 12,500±130 years ago (Mo-441) and contains slab-lined hearths, distinctive antler harpoons, and many fish remains, reflecting the beginnings of the fishery that was to be an important aspect of economic life in the area from this time on.

A rather different picture is presented by the 1968–69 excavations in Diuktai Cave in the middle Aldan valley, far to the north. Here mammoth and muskox remains were associated with bifacial stone spear and dart points, burins, blades, wedge-shaped and disc-shaped cores, and skreblos. Of greatest interest, of course, are the bifacial points; with the exception of the lost specimens from the Irkutsk Military Hospital, these are the only such points of indubitable Pleistocene age known in Siberia. They may trace back to pre-Aurignacoid influence or migration from the South Russian Plain, where this general type of point was characteristic in much earlier times. And they are of particular importance for the problem of New World origins, to be discussed presently. For this reason the radiocarbon dates from Diuktai Cave are disappointingly late: 13,070±90 (LE–784) and 12,090±120 (LE–860). However, the excavator, IU. A. Mochanov, believes that the cave assemblage represents the final stage of a persistent cultural tradition in the Aldan region which is reflected at other sites as well. One of these, Verkhne-Troitskaia, is in a geologically older context — but whether as old as the 20–25,000 years postulated by Mochanov is problematical. Results of the continuing work at these sites will be awaited with interest.

Since the rather crude heavy tools so conspicuous especially on later sites are thought to reflect woodworking, we might expect them to be lacking

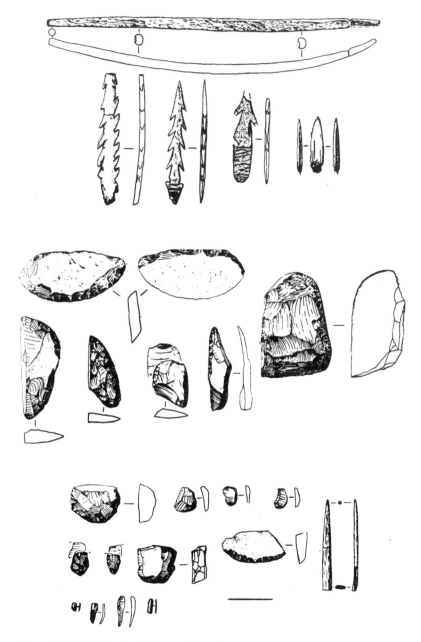

Figure 1.20. Verkholenskaia Gora: artifacts from the lowest level (III) (after Aksenov).

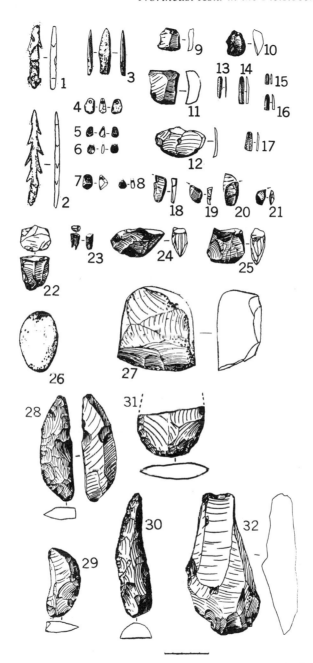

Figure 1.21. Verkholenskaia Gora: artifacts from level II. 1, 2 — antler harpoons; 19, 21 — transverse burins; 24, 25 — wedge-shaped cores; 28–30 — knives; 31 — base of a point; 32 — adze-like tool (after Aksenov).

Figure 1.22. Verkholenskaia Gora: three types of harpoons (photograph by Roger Powers).

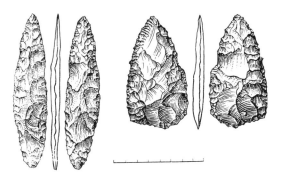

Figure 1.23. Bifacial points from Diuktai Cave (after Mochanov).

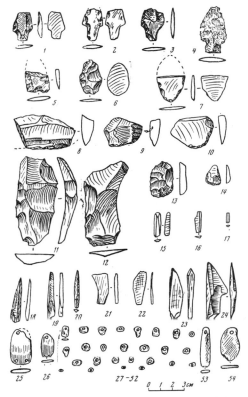

Figure 1.24. Ushki: artifacts from the Palaeolithic level.
Numbers 18–54 are from the burial (after Dikov).

among any group living in a wholly tundra environment. This is the case at
the only tundra site of Pleistocene age in Siberia — Ushki Lake in Kamchatka. The lowest horizon here (VII) with dates of 13,600±250 (GIN–167)
and 14,300±200 years (according to the excavator, N. N. Dikov[8]) contains a
purely small-tool technology including tanged arrowpoints that resemble nothing elsewhere. This level has been excavated over 180 square meters,
revealing twelve hearths and a burial from which the human remains had
completely decomposed as a result of ground water. However, the grave
contained red ocher, artifacts, pendants, and numerous stone beads which had
evidently been sewn on the clothing of the deceased. A somewhat different
later stage of culture belonging to the terminal Pleistocene is represented in
levels V, VA, and VI, but also confined largely to small tools, including
elongated bifacial foliate arrow points, bifacial knives, Gobi cores, ski spalls,

8. An earlier determination of 21,200±900 (GIN–186) is now generally rejected as errone-
ous.

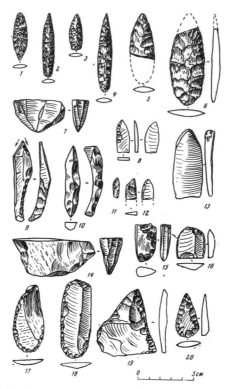

Figure 1.25. Ushki: artifacts from levels v and vi (after Dikov).

and microblades. Prismatic blade cores are lacking and burins very rare. The complex has no analogies elsewhere as a whole, but Dikov sees a number of individual trait parallels with such late sites as Kokorevo III on the Yenisei and Fediaevo on the Angara. This is consonant with a radiocarbon date of 10,360±350 B.P. (Mo-345) for level v. (The bifacial points are also reminiscent of the Osipovka site on the Amur.) Of particular interest was the discovery of the remains of seven dwellings, two of them shallow pits, rectangular, round, or oval in plan and twelve to twenty square meters in size, which are ascribed by the excavator to level vi. The complex stratigraphic problems encountered at Ushki suggest caution in assigning and interpreting the finds from this site.

The Anangula site in the Aleutians is considered by Müller-Beck to reflect a late survival of the Aurignacoid technical tradition which either entered Alaska at the very close of the Pleistocene or perhaps represented the surviving population of the Bering Land Bridge. In either case it would suggest the presence of a tundra-adapted population in extreme northeastern Siberia dur-

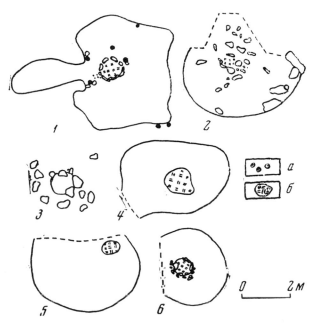

Figure 1.26. Ushki: remains of dwellings ascribed to level vɪ. Numbers 1 and 6 are shallow pits. Key: *a*—post holes; *b*—hearth (after Dikov).

ing the late Pleistocene whose culture lacked the typical features of the forest-zone Siberian Palaeolithic and preserved to a great extent the traditions of the original Aurignacoid migrants from eastern Europe. On this basis we may postulate the existence of still another regional manifestation of Pleistocene culture in interior Siberia.

The Soviet Far East and Korea, as we pointed out, have at all times provided a different environment from the interior, as well as being separated by geographical barriers. It is not surprising that the late Pleistocene cultural remains here differ markedly from those of the subarctic periglacial hunting cultures which we have been discussing. Unfortunately, the evidence as yet is very limited.

The few assemblages reflect a monotonous technology lacking diagnostic artifacts — a situation conducive to overemphasis on any trait that seems at all distinctive. In general, researchers put great dependence on technological traditions of tool manufacture in their historical interpretations, so that cores receive far more attention than the tools themselves. In the Soviet Far East at least, no bone is preserved (except in the one cave site), and there is no basis for dating any of the evidence: no radiocarbon dates as yet, no palaeontological remains, and only subjective guesses from the geologists.

Of uncertain age but possibly as old as Early Würm is the lowest level at

the stratified Coulpo (Kulp'o) site in northeastern North Korea, the first
Korean Palaeolithic site. Here what the excavators believe to be the remains
of a dwelling and workshop were uncovered associated with artifacts of
quartzite: choppers, cores, and scrapers and pointed tools made on flakes that
seem to fall into the general technological tradition of Choukoutien and the
Fenho sites in North China. An overlying level, evidently of late Pleistocene
age, contained a somewhat different complex of flakes and cores made of sil-
icified shale. Both levels had to some extent suffered disturbance from a later
Neolithic occupation. Materials of late Pleistocene type occur more abundantly at another site five kilometers away. Although so far known only from
the surface, it is hoped that further work may locate an intact portion of the
occupation layer here. Unfortunately only scanty information is available
about these obviously important finds.

Somewhat the same picture seems to be provided by recently investigated
sites at Sokchang-ni in South Korea. Here underlying levels are said to have
produced tools reminiscent of North Chinese industries and perhaps roughly
comparable in time to the early horizons at Hoshino and Iwajuku in Japan.
Upper levels, one said to have been dated at 20,825 ± 1880 B.P., yielded what
are described as ''Aurignacian-like'' tools. Details are lacking, and for the
present Korea still contributes little to our understanding of Pleistocene developments in East Asia. The rugged geography of the peninsula leads one to
suspect that much of the record may be submerged beneath the present sea on
former coastal plains.

The Palaeolithic in the Soviet Far East is best represented at the Osinovka
site, where it is associated with a stratum of red soil believed to represent a
warmer climate than the present. This is overlain by diluvial material thought
to reflect a cold period. Thus the level is considered to belong to an interstadial, probably in the later phases of the final glaciation. Higher levels at the
site contain ''Mesolithic'' and later materials. Okladnikov sees the
Palaeolithic occupants as the northernmost link in a chain of Southeast Asian
hunting-gathering forest cultures of the late Palaeolithic and Mesolithic,
reflecting an ecological pattern of small-mammal hunting and plant gathering
which he feels is similar to the picture at the Upper Cave of Choukoutien. Just
as in the Indo-Chinese peninsula, in Okladnikov's view, a very ancient technical tradition based on chopper and skreblo-like tools made from whole
pebbles persisted into quite recent times. He feels the Osinovka complex to be
roughly contemporary with the late Palaeolithic of Siberia and Mongolia.
Tool types include distinctive almond-shaped artifacts said to be reminiscent
of Acheulean handaxes (but only in a very general and approximate sense)
and core-like chopping tools likewise reminiscent to some extent of Southeast
Asian choppers. Though in general appearance both types seem very archaic,
there are blade facets on some of the core-like tools that reflect much more

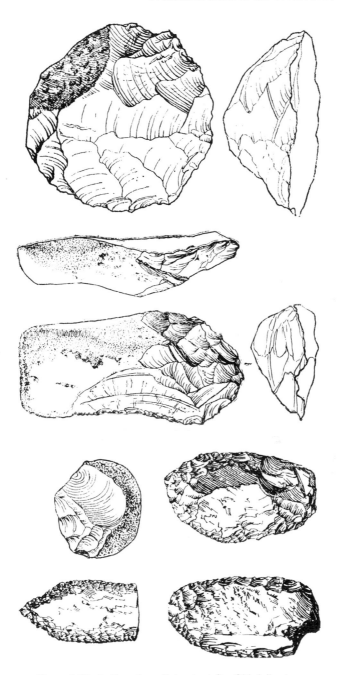

Figure 1.27. Artifacts from Osinovka (after Okladnikov).

advanced techniques. Also, these types are associated with artifacts made on more or less regular blades.

Recent and as yet unpublished investigations at Kumara on the Middle Amur have recovered bona fide pebble tools (fig. 1.28) in situ at considerable depth in a loam horizon which are said to be very similar to comparable artifacts at Moil'tyn-am in Mongolia. Also present are prepared-platform and sub-prismatic blade cores and skreblos. Doubtless primarily on typological grounds the Kumara finds are assigned to the same general time horizon as Osinovka.

Indubitable Upper Pleistocene age can be assigned only to the scanty finds in the Geographical Society Cave near Nakhodka (Vladivostok area), where a prepared-platform core and pebbles treated with side blows were associated with mammoth.

Soviet prehistorians working in the Far East see two basic technological traditions in the region that persist into the early Holocene and in fact form the basis for contrasting early Neolithic complexes that later developed. One, based on pebbles, features an important increment of heavy tools. The other is characterized by an evolutionary development of prepared-platform cores which in the Soviet literature are labeled "pro-Levallois," "Levallois," "epi-Levallois," etc. These terms should be understood as purely descriptive, denoting platform preparation, and not as implying any relationship with the true Levallois technique of the West. They are seen as a local, parallel development in East Asia, which eventually evolved through crude prototype

Figure 1.28. Pebble tools from Kumara ii (photograph by Roger Powers).

stages into prismatic blade cores — a process already noted in Mongolia. The developmental stages are seen as reflected at Kumara and in the Palaeolithic horizon at Osinovka (Osinovka I). Full flowering of this local blade technique is to be seen in the overlying Osinovka II horizon and the almost identical Ustinovka (Tadusha) workshop site, considered to be terminal Pleistocene on the basis of stratigraphic position and parallels with Hokkaido. Ustinovka yielded a variety of prepared platform cores (e.g., fig. 1.29), with blanks for Gobi cores (a distinctive type of wedge-shaped microblade core) being the most numerous. All tools were made on blades.

To supplement the archaeological data, certain inferences regarding mainland Northeast Asia at this period may be drawn from Pleistocene geography.

The topography of Northeast Asia, with a rugged mountain barrier walling off the Pacific watershed from the interior, creates two distinct funnels for animals or man from continental Eurasia to the New World. The northern funnel, at its apex, would have involved tundra conditions even in optimum climatic periods, as far as we can tell. Thus it would have been provided with an effective filter: only those animals and human groups adapted to tundra life could have passed through it, though for those so equipped it was always passable, at least as far as the present shores of Bering Strait. By its nature it would have drawn its migrants from the great northern plain of Eurasia, which physiographically stretches west to the North Sea and south to the Middle East, though we may assume that the odds would favor tundra-adapted groups

Figure 1.29. "Epi-levallois" core from Ustinovka (photograph by Roger Powers).

in interior Siberia. The pacific coastal funnel would have drawn from the Amur basin, Japan, Manchuria, Korea, and North China. However, it would only have been feasible during times of lowered sea level, when the narrow coastal shelf along the Sea of Okhotsk between the Amur and Kamchatka was available. Otherwise, as at the present day, the precipitous coast is impassable to the land traveler. At the same time, we must presuppose availability of this stretch during times favorable for tree growth; otherwise it would be hard to visualize a northward movement of the forest- and forest-steppe-adapted population of eastern Asia.

With lowered sea levels, large areas would have been added to the tundra zone of Northeast Asia — in particular Beringia (the Bering Platform) and the continental shelf lying north of the present arctic coast of Siberia. Topographically, these areas would have been more favorable for animals and man than the rugged land mass presently above water. It is thus highly likely that the bulk of early human occupation of extreme northeastern Asia was in areas now submerged, with the corollary that most of the archaeological record may be lost beyond recovery. We must bear this in mind in assessing negative evidence from this region.

During those times when Beringia and Alaska were an extension of Asia, cut off from North America by the Canadian ice barrier, they may have held Asiatic populations and industries which might not necessarily have proceeded farther into the New World subsequently. We must therefore expect to find remains in this region which are alien to the New World.

As for actual archaeological evidence in mainland Northeast Asia that might throw light on the Old World roots of the early New World cultures, it can only be said that this has yet to be found. Parallels can always be pointed out in some scattered traits — none of which are old enough in Siberia to be relevant — but there are no known traditions or complexes which could serve as antecedents. Particularly lacking are any roots for the great efflorescence of bifacial projectile points so characteristic of the New World scene. Perhaps the rare instances of Siberian bifacial points, as at Diuktai Cave, are survivals of an earlier tradition yet to be discovered on Siberian soil, whose antecedents trace back to sites on the South Russian plain such as Kostenki, as Müller-Beck has hypothesized. For the present, the problem of New World origins remains as enigmatic as ever.

Japan, because of its geographical position relative to the mainland and its history of alternating isolation and contact with it, offers a unique laboratory — a virtual test tube — for studying the processes of cultural evolution and culture change in human societies under relatively controlled conditions. As such it should be of interest to cultural anthropologists in general and not just to archaeologists; but the possibilities from this point of view have not yet been realized. Because the two main points of contact with the mainland lie at opposite ends of the long island arc, each links up with a very different cultural sphere of East Asia. Japan is thus a meeting place of influences from north and south whose ramifications reach as far away as Europe and north-western North America on the one hand and Southeast Asia on the other.

During the final glaciation, as noted earlier, Hokkaido formed part of Siberia while the remaining islands (a single land mass) were very briefly connected to or accessible from the mainland at either end, judging by faunal and cultural evidence. Presumably this occurred around 18,000 years ago. Until then, the main islands had been a refuge area, as illustrated by the survival of an archaic form of elephant, *Paleoloxodon*, in Honshu long after its disappearance on the mainland. In general, the main islands are charac-terized by a loess fauna like that of North China, although the vegetation was mixed forest. The North Eurasian mammoth fauna, with few exceptions, is confined to the boreal environment of Hokkaido. The present Inland Sea and coastal shelves were dry land, and would have made up a substantial part of the total lowland area of Japan at that time. Thus any evidence of man's exploitation of the coastal zone — so typical of Japan from its first surviving traces — is lost under the present sea, as well as the record in much of what must have been the most favorable areas for human occupancy.

The basis for relative, and in a few cases absolute, dating of late Pleis-tocene remains in Japan is the stratigraphic sequence of so-called "loam" deposits which are considered to represent volcanic ash. This provides good sequences in many localities but they involve only a limited area. The basic chronological problem is the difficulty in correlating sequences between dif-ferent areas, and thus in establishing firm temporal relationships between sites on a more than local basis. Between widely separated areas, such correlations (and datings) are sheer guess work. Radiocarbon dating as an aid is hampered by the absence of organic materials in archaeological sites; in a few cases it has provided ages for relevant geological horizons. As in Siberia, the great majority of sites seem to date from the last half of the final glaciation. Stratified sites are rare. All in all, it is not possible to give a sequential picture of cultural development and culture history in Japan at this time. Our evi-dence, furthermore, must be regarded as a biased sample. Most Pleistocene sites are on hill slopes, where they have been able to escape obliteration from intensive agriculture. Between the effects of the latter and the rising sea levels, we must assume that a major, and probably the most typical, part of the record is not available to us. We may be basing our inferences on the atypical.

Despite the great number of late Pleistocene sites discovered in the past twenty years, they provide a disappointingly poor picture of human activity, yielding as they do nothing but stone tool assemblages. Typical sites are small, with no indication of protracted residence — but we must realize that

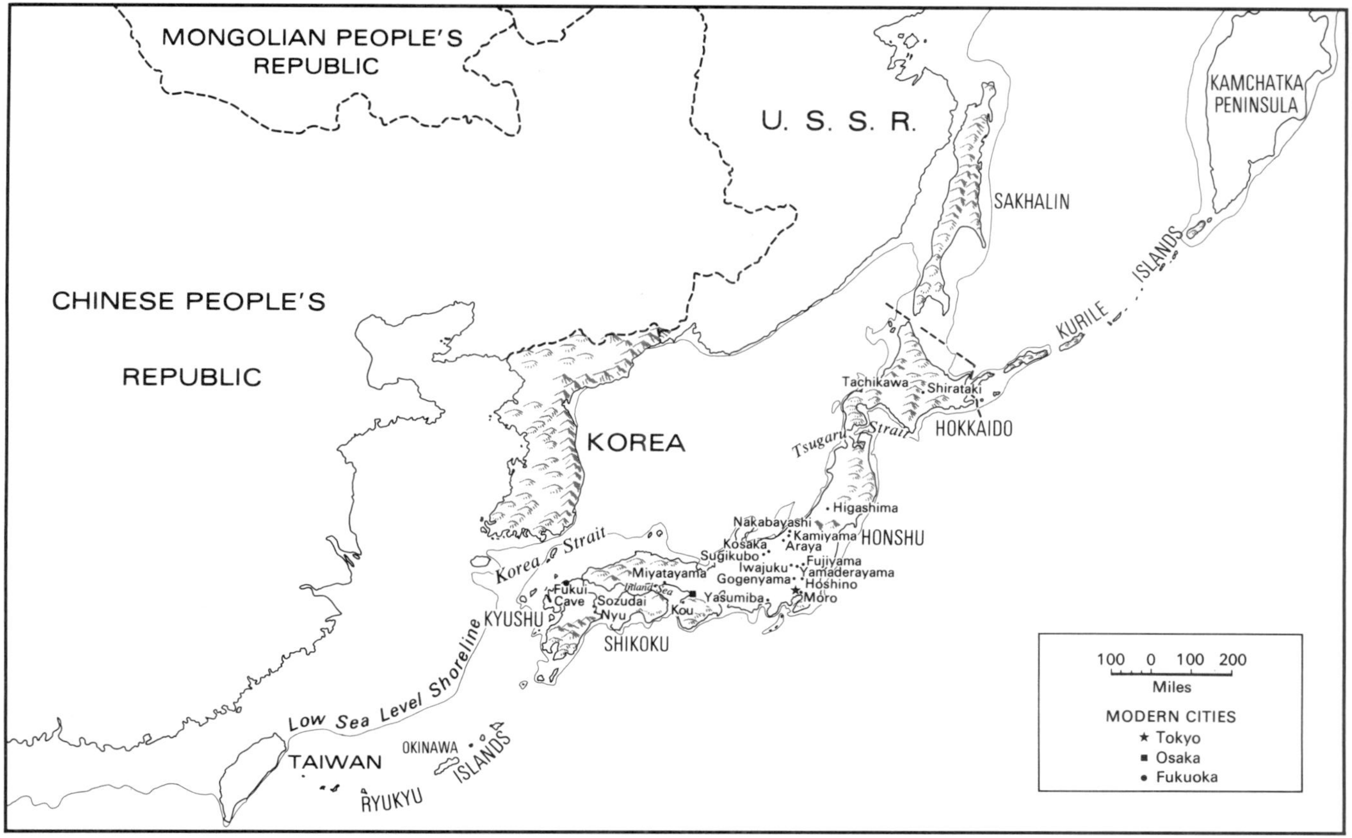
MONGOLIAN PEOPLE'S
REPUBLIC
U. S. S. R.
KAMCHATKA
PENINSULA
SAKHALIN
KURILE ISLANDS
CHINESE PEOPLE'S
REPUBLIC
KOREA
Tachikawa
Shirataki
HOKKAIDO
Tsugaru Strait
Higashima
Nakabayashi
Kamiyama
HONSHU
Kosaka
Araya
Sugikubo
Fujiyama
Iwajuku
Yamaderayama
Gogenyama
Hoshino
Miyatayama
Korea Strait
Fukui
Cave
Inland Sea
Yasumiba
Moro
Sozudai
Nyu
Kou
KYUSHU
SHIKOKU
Low Sea Level Shoreline
OKINAWA
TAIWAN
RYUKYU
ISLANDS
100 0 100 200
Miles
MODERN CITIES
★ Tokyo
■ Osaka
• Fukuoka

Map 2. Preceramic Japan.

University of Wisconsin Cartographic Laboratory

such possibly marginal locations may have been only seasonal or occupational facies of the total culture. Japan offers nothing like the data available from a few good sites in Siberia or other regions where fewer remains may actually yield more information. In most cases there is a lack of any patterned relationship of the archaeological materials, let alone the lack of living sites in any real sense. Ecological data are completely absent. Thus our knowledge of even the total technology of the late Pleistocene is severely limited, while that of human ecology and behavior is virtually nil.

The general simplicity, even crudity, of most assemblages as compared with those of contemporary Europe or even Siberia creates a doubtless misleading impression of cultural underdevelopment: we have no way of knowing the level and complexity of the bone and wood technology that must have been associated. From analogies elsewhere, this may well have been impressive: skilled woodcarving can be done with only the simplest of stone cutting tools. For the prehistorian, the lack of diagnostic artifact types makes standard comparative studies difficult. The true nature and significance of such types as can be recognized is not clear: are they functional (and hence ultimately ecological) or do they simply reflect cultural traditions?

The Pleistocene (more commonly called ''preceramic'') archaeological materials in Japan have been traditionally forced into a classification of four major hypothetical ''cultures'' of dubious validity and even less convincing temporal succession. But it is scarcely possible to speak of more than certain persisting technological traditions (i.e., traditionally transmitted concepts of artifact production) which occur in various combinations. These combinations of shared technical traits may prove to be valid cultural complexes, but it seems premature to describe those proposed so far in a work of this nature. Basically, the entire ''preceramic'' stone technology represents variants of an industry with predominant reliance on blades or elongate flakes. Retouch is almost exclusively confined to one face and usually is applied only along the margins. Heavy tools are scarce and occasional. There is no reflection in Japan of the late Pleistocene efflorescence of heavy tools in mainland Northeast Asia. Perhaps this did not take place until the time when sea levels had risen sufficiently to isolate the islands once more.

Classic blade technique, probably a result of influences from the Aurignacoid tradition of northern Eurasia, was confined to the north — Hokkaido and northern Honshu. Obviously it entered from Siberia. Its area of distribution coincides with the probable extent of the boreal forest zone during the Würm maximum. Typically it is associated with well-developed techniques for the manufacture of burins, which suggests major reliance on bone as a raw material (another Aurignacoid characteristic) although evidence of this cannot be expected to have survived.

The temperate forest zone of the rest of Japan based its technology on

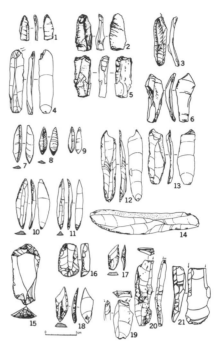

Figure 1.30. Typical blade tools from preceramic sites. 1–6 — Kamiyama-type burins; 7–11 — Sugikubo-type knives; 12–14 — Higashi-yama-type knives; 15, 16 — end scrapers; 17, 18 — backed knives; 19–21 — Kosaka-type burins. Scale approximate (after S. Sugihara, ed., *Nihon no Kokogaku*, vol. 1, with permission).

elongate flakes, a tradition either of indigenous origin or introduced through the southern end of the islands from the adjacent mainland. They provided blanks for a variety of artifacts, including several knife forms. Burins in any significant number are lacking here, reflecting the lesser use of bone that might be expected in this area. The Inland Sea region in particular is characterized by the distinctive side-blow technique of producing flakes (which has been likened to slicing a loaf of French bread) — a development perhaps initially traceable to the nature of the raw material available, sanukite.

Towards the end of the Pleistocene, two conspicuous developments appear: an efflorescence of bifacial projectile points and microblade technology. The former may be an entirely indigenous development reflecting a shift to projectile hunting weapons, since bifacial leaf-shaped artifacts are frequently associated with elongate flakes in the southern zone. (They do not derive from the northern blade tradition.) These appear to have evolved into stemmed points in central Japan and to have subsequently diffused both north and south — a specialized development that occurred just at the time when pottery was making its first appearance. There are no stemmed points in mainland North-

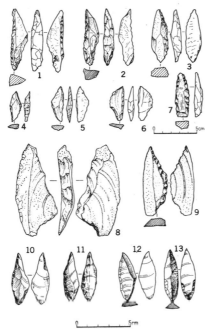

Figure 1.31. Examples of tools made on elongate flakes from preceramic sites. 1–7 — Miyatayama-type knives (made on side-blow flakes); 8, 9 — Kou-type knives (made on side-blow flakes); 10–13 — Moro-type knives (made on end-blow flakes). Numbers 8 and 9 not to scale (no. 8 is approximately seven centimeters in length) (after Sugihara, ed., *Nihon no Kokogaku*, vol. 1, with permission).

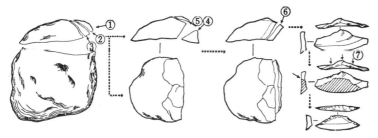

Figure 1.32. Reconstruction of the Setouchi technique of side-blow flaking (after Sugihara, ed., *Nihon no Kokogaku*, vol. 1, with permission).

east Asia until very much later, if we except the few enigmatic specimens from Ushki in Kamchatka, which bear no resemblance.

The origins and history of microblade technology in Japan are a subject of heated controversy and conflicting opinion. There are at least two distinct technical traditions involved, in terms of manufacturing techniques. One, primarily northern in distribution, is based on wedge-shaped cores and is

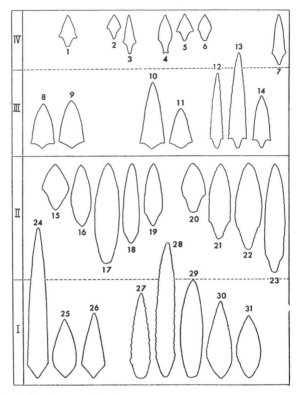

Figure 1.33. Evolution of stemmed points as proposed by C. Serizawa (after Serizawa, with permission).

obviously related to the widespread manifestations of this technique in mainland Northeast Asia, entering by way of Hokkaido. The other, generally characterized by conical or cylindrical cores, may have evolved in Japan out of the earlier blade tradition. Both in any case reflect a need for small tools, probably often for use in composite artifacts, that is widespread in the Old World at this general time horizon.

The general impression conveyed by the late Pleistocene ("preceramic") archaeological materials is one of development in isolation. There was some cultural influence from the north (Siberia-Hokkaido), but it was limited and did not penetrate very far into the main island. The possibility existed for comparable or greater influence from the south, but the situation is difficult to evaluate since we know virtually nothing about the adjoining mainland (South Korea-North China) at this time period. Only about 13,000 years ago did the outside world begin to impinge significantly. Within Japan, regional differences are discernible, but we do not know what they signify — whether different cultural traditions or different ecological adaptations. The latter

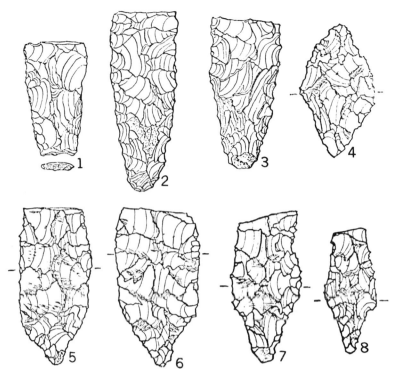

Figure 1.34. Bifacial point types from the Nakabayashi site. 1–3 — leaf-shaped; 4–6 — shouldered; 7, 8 — stemmed (after Serizawa, with permission).

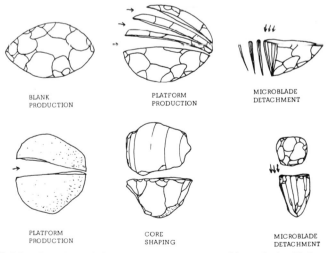

Figure 1.35. Manufacturing techniques underlying the two traditions of microblade technology, characterized by wedge-shaped or primarily conical cores (after Kobayashi).

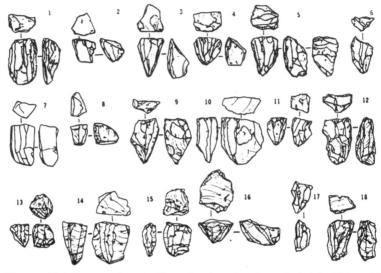

Figure 1.36. Microcores from the Yasumiba site (primarily conical) (after Kobayashi).

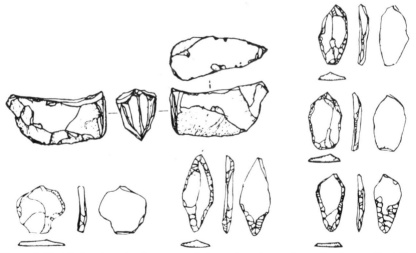

Figure 1.37. Wedge-shaped microcore and Araya-type burins from the Araya site (after Kobayashi).

would be quite expectable, especially in view of the marked environmental contrasts between north and south.

Hokkaido was at all times and in every way a different world from the rest of Japan and must be viewed separately. This appendage of Siberia had an essentially periglacial climate during the final glaciation, with forests perhaps retreating to the coasts, leaving the highlands open country. The latter might have been suitable for plains-adapted hunters of Siberian type, an intriguing possibility.

There is no indication that Hokkaido was occupied by man prior to the Würm maximum. The oldest known site is possibly 20,000 years. The chronology of subsequent culture history is based on remains associated with

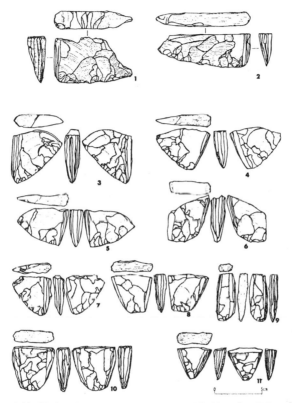

Figure 1.38. Wedge-shaped microcores from Hokkaido (after Kobayashi).

a series of river terraces in the Shirataki valley on which a few radiocarbon and obsidian hydration datings have been obtained. There is no other relevant geological stratigraphy elsewhere, no stratified sites nor absolute dates; problems of temporal relationships are thus much more difficult than on the main island. Technologically, Pleistocene Hokkaido could be viewed as a local special development of the Aurignacoid technology of Siberia. Widespread microcore techniques are conspicuous. The general impression is one of cultural continuity on the island through time with successive technological changes in major tool types; in other words, evolution within a single basic technological tradition. The only significant intrusion from outside is the appearance at the very end of the period of bifacial projectile points from the main island.

Bibliography

Aksenov, M. P.
  1969. "Archaeological Investigations at the Stratified Site of Verkholens-kaia Gora in 1963–1965." *Arctic Anthropology* 6, no. 1: 74–87.
Dikov, N. N..
  1968. "The Discovery of the Palaeolithic in Kamchatka and the Problem of the Initial Occupation of America." *Arctic Anthropology* 5, no. 1: 191–203.
Frenzel, Burkhard
  1968. "The Pleistocene Vegetation of Northern Eurasia." *Science* 161: 637–49.
Gabori, Miklos
  1964. "New Data on Palaeolithic Finds in Mongolia." *Asian Perspectives* 7: 105–12.
Hopkins, David M., ed.
  1967. *The Bering Land Bridge.* Stanford: Stanford University Press.
Irving, William N.
  1971. "Recent Early Man Research in the North." *Arctic Anthropology* 8, no. 2: 68–82.
Istoriia Sibiri [*History of Siberia*].
  1968. Vol. 1. Leningrad: Nauka.
Klein, Richard G.
  1971. "The Pleistocene Prehistory of Siberia." *Quaternary Research* 1: 133–61.
Kobayashi, Tatsuo
  1970. "Microblade Industries in the Japanese Archipelago." *Arctic Anthropology* 7, no. 2: 38–58.
Kotani, Yoshinobu
  1969. "Upper Pleistocene and Holocene Environmental Conditions in Japan." *Arctic Anthropology* 5, no. 2: 133–58.
Larichev, V. E.
  1969. *Paleolit Severnoi, Tsentral'noi i Vostochnoi Azii.* [*The Palaeolithic of Northern, Central and Eastern Asia*]. Novosibirsk: Nauka, Sibirskoe Otdelenie.
———, and Grigorenko, B. G.
  1969. "The Discovery of the Palaeolithic in Korea." *Arctic Anthropology* 6, no. 1: 128–33.
Medvedev, G. I.
  1969. "Archaeological Investigations of the Stratified Palaeolithic Site of

Krasnyi IAr on the Angara in 1964–65." *Arctic Anthropology* 6, no. 1: 30–44.

Michael, Henry N., ed.
　　1964. *The Archaeology and Geomorphology of Northern Asia: Selected Works.* Toronto: University of Toronto Press.
Morlan, Richard E.
　　1967a. "The Preceramic Period of Hokkaido." *Arctic Anthropology* 4, no. 1: 164–220.
　　1967b. "Chronometric Dating in Japan." *Arctic Anthropology* 4, no. 2: 180–211.
Morlan, Valda J.
　　1971. "The Preceramic Period of Japan: Honshu, Shikoku and Kyushu." *Arctic Anthropology* 8, no. 1: 136–70.
Müller-Beck, Hansjürgen
　　1967. "On Migrations of Hunters Across the Bering Land Bridge in the Upper Pleistocene." In *The Bering Land Bridge*, edited by David M. Hopkins, pp. 373–408. Stanford: Stanford University Press.
Okladnikov, A. P.
　　1965. *The Soviet Far East in Antiquity.* Toronto: University of Toronto Press.
　　1969. "An Ancient Settlement on the Tadusha River at Ustinovka and the Problem of the Far Eastern Mesolithic." *Arctic Anthropology* 6, no. 1: 134–49.
Powers, William Roger
　　1973. "Palaeolithic Man in Northeast Asia." *Arctic Anthropology* 10, no. 2.
Shutler, Richard, Jr., ed.
　　1971. "Papers from a Symposium on Early Man in North America, New Developments: 1960–1970." *Arctic Anthropology* 8, no. 2: 1–91.
Wormington, H. M.
　　1974. *Ancient Hunters and Gatherers of the Americas: the Archaeological Record Before 6000 B.C.* New York: Academic Press.

2 Neolithic Siberia and Its Near Neighbors

The postglacial hiatus in the prehistory of Europe, seen by nineteenth-century prehistorians, has had its counterpart in mainland Northeast Asia. The publishings of these prehistorians reflected a virtual blank between the latest Palaeolithic and the first ceramic cultures which universally here carry the label "Neolithic." No remains have until recently been known which indubitably fit in between the two periods, though some have been advanced from time to time. As a result, the early Holocene is by far the least known period in the human history of mainland Northeast Asia: with a few exceptions archaeological materials are of dubious attribution or virtually unpublished, and human remains from what was doubtless a crucial period of population movement and rearrangement are totally lacking.

There has been considerable argument as to whether the concept of a "Mesolithic" can even be applied in this part of the world. In Siberia, Palaeolithic cultures persist into the early Holocene, as we have seen, and opinion has favored a direct evolution into the earliest Neolithic. The recent discovery of sites apparently of intermediate age has done nothing to alter the picture, and the terms "Epipalaeolithic" or "Holocene Palaeolithic" have been proposed as the most suitable descriptive labels for many of these.

To briefly sketch the postglacial environmental conditions, the period from c. 10,000 to 8000 years ago is described as "moderately cold" — perhaps not too different from the present. The spread of the taiga from its glacial refugium to approximately its present distribution and the return of the mixed forest to the Amur basin were completed by the end of this time, presenting man with a modern environment, modern fauna, and present sea levels and geography. We do not know to what extent these vegetation changes were already under way in Late Sartan times; certainly the warm phase corresponding to the Alleröd of Europe must have evoked some response. But even so, this wholesale transformation of the vegetation of northern Eurasia must have taken place within a span of no more than 4000 years at the most, and much of it in shorter segments than that. Considering the vast areas involved, it was an explosive process and must have had sudden and major effects on the animal biota (extinctions of megafauna?) and on man. The fact that our limited body of archaeological data from this time comes largely from the southern fringe of Siberia, where there was little essential change in the environment, may help to explain the area's apparent cultural continuity — so different from the changing picture in contemporary Europe, which was faced with recovery from actual glaciation and ultimate transition to a temperate mixed forest. Here, no major technological readjustment was necessary.

The postglacial climatic optimum is an appropriate term to use in Siberia for the period c. 8000–4500 B.P. The climate was warmer than today, and the vegetation zones spread north of their present limits. On the lower Lena, for instance, spruce and pine pollen occurs several hundred kilometers north of its present range, and trunks of birch trees of normal size and of willows ten to thirteen centimeters in diameter have been found in peat deposits. Still farther north, on the New Siberian Islands, there is evidence of larch, birch, and grass. This is not considered to represent actual forest cover in these far northern areas, but rather the presence of forest tundra (wooded tundra) and tongues of forest in the river valleys. By analogy elsewhere, we may suspect that Mongolia was less inviting for human habitation and that large areas were abandoned completely at this time. The maximum Holocene transgression of the sea must coincide with some part of this period, although raised strand lines in eastern Siberia 10 meters above present sea level, apparently attributed to this time, must be primarily due to tectonic activity. Thus, although environmental conditions in Northeast Asia during the climatic optimum may have invited northward movement of population, movement along the Pacific coast and contact with offshore areas, if such occurred, must have been by water.

By about 4000 years ago, a cooler climate like that of the present was already setting in.

Early Holocene sites in Siberia occur in the same areas that reveal traces of Pleistocene man: the upper middle Yenisei valley, the upper Angara, upper Lena and Aldan valleys, Trans-Baikal, the Maritime Territory, and Kamchatka. Again, the areal distribution may be presumed to reflect accessibility to modern investigators as much as the actual distribution of early Holocene human populations. There are a fair number of evidently contemporary sites in Mongolia, some possible ones in Manchuria, but nothing as yet in Korea. In view of the cultural developments taking place in Japan at this time, we may assume that far more evidence of human activity on the adjacent mainland will be forthcoming.

The limited and gradual environmental changes in southern interior Siberia made it possible for the late Palaeolithic culture and ecological pattern to persist with only minor adaptations and changes. Thus the early postglacial sites have traditionally been included within the Siberian Palaeolithic.

A pattern of mixed economy with relatively stable occupation of favorable locations was evidently established in the interior quite early in the Holocene, probably as the landscape returned to forest. This pattern was to persist until quite recent times. With purely forest game animals available (solitary), fishing became of major importance. Hunting remained the dominant resource only on the tundra, with its large herds of reindeer. Particular cultural features vary with regions, usually due to continuity from the particular local ancestor, but also suggesting a number of local adaptations in situ with some diffusion of traits. The geometric microlithic technique so characteristic of Europe at this time was completely absent from Siberia.

Spanning this time period is the remarkable Ust'-Belaia site on the upper Angara, where sixteen horizons have been identified, down to the Neolithic. The site lies entirely within the Holocene, and contains only a forest fauna. At each stage the picture suggests a large, long-term settlement — evidently a base camp for a hunting group. The original human occupation of this inviting spot where the Belaia River debouches into the Angara occurred when the present first terrace was still a part of the flood plain. Only some 10 percent of the total area of this rich site has as yet been uncovered, but this has yielded forty hearths and thousands of artifacts.

The inventory, both stone and bone, is numerous and diverse, showing more diversity than any other settlement of this time range in Siberia. Although the familiar choppers and skreblos persist, they form a small fraction of the total and diminish with time, unlike the picture at contemporary Yenisei sites. The prismatic blade technique is highly developed, and blades make up the commonest lithic category, occurring in all sizes. They were used principally as side blades in composite tools and also as arrow points. In the latter case they were only slightly retouched at tip or base, in a fashion reminiscent of the Swiderian points of eastern Europe or those found in the famous Khinskaia Ravine burial in this same area. In addition there are bifacial arrow and spear points. Slotted bone and antler dart points, knives, and so on have their closest analogies in such late Palaeolithic Trans-Baikal sites as Oshurkovo and Zarubino. A few polished stone tools occur. Slate bayonets like those in the Khinskaia burial are stated to have been found in "the main Mesolithic horizon," while a nephrite adze with only the edge ground and two polished slate tools were associated in a pit with "Mesolithic artifacts" (unspecified), so that their stratigraphic provenience is considered to be firmly established. Other finds at Ust'-Belaia include what are considered the oldest fish spears (leisters) and compound hooks in Siberia, also the earliest mother-of-pearl beads. All are characteristic features of later periods on the Angara. The dog was also present, as shown by a ritual burial older than 9000 years. From the fact that Ust'-Belaia, like the few other comparable sites of the area, shows a combination of Palaeolithic survivals with first appearances of subsequent Neolithic traits, but little that is distinctive of this segment of time alone, the term "Epipalaeolithic" is being increasingly applied to such transitional settlements.

A comparable span is reflected in the Sumnagin culture of the Aldan River, which the excavator, IU. A. Mochanov, has labeled "Holocene Palaeolithic." Here 90 percent of the tools are made on blades taken from prismatic cores with no trace of bifacial working. Most are microtools: insert blades for composite artifacts, burins, perforators, scrapers. Less than 10 percent of the assemblage comprises heavy tools made on pebbles, such as skreblos, chopping tools, axes, and adzes. There are some slotted bone artifacts but no trace of the use of the bow and arrow. The Sumnagin culture is said to be distinctive and unlike anything else in Siberia at this time level. The dozen sites investigated were temporary camps of hunters of moose and reindeer.

In northern Asia it is customary to begin the Neolithic with the appearance of pottery. However, assemblages are encountered which contain all essential elements of the local Neolithic with the exception of pottery and which, for

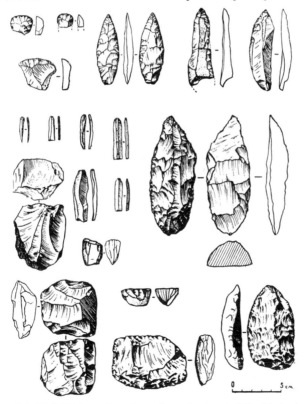

Figure 2.1. Ust'-Belaia: artifacts from the earliest levels (after Medvedev).

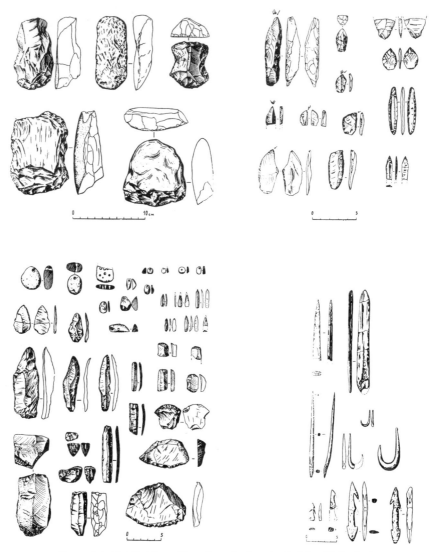

Figure 2.2. Ust'-Belaia: artifacts from the later levels (after Medvedev).

one reason or another, are thought to be older. The term "preceramic Neolithic" has been applied to these assemblages by a number of writers, and they are viewed as the final stage of the postglacial transition period. The lowest level of the famous Ulan Khada site on the shores of Lake Baikal has been advanced by some as a stratigraphically controlled example of such a stage, and disputed by others. Most such assemblages reported to date lack such control and the attribution is primarily typological. In defense of the concept of a "preceramic Neolithic" — which may seem a contradiction in terms — it has been argued that groups which had settled down to a sedentary fishing economy may have adopted pottery sooner than otherwise identical groups which pursued a more roving hunting existence.

Postglacial remains from the Pacific coast are as distinctive and as dissimilar from interior Siberia as was the case in the Pleistocene. The persistence of two earlier technical traditions has already been noted in Chapter 1, with full flowering of the blade technique at the Ustinovka (Tadusha) workshop site, assigned to the terminal Pleistocene. The workshop is thought to have continued in use into the early Holocene with no essential change. The lower, preceramic level at the Maikhe site, also in the southern part of the Maritime Territory, which underlies a Neolithic settlement, continues the blade tradition and is likewise viewed as early Holocene, primarily on the basis of the stage of development of the blade technique. However, also present are diagonal burins of the type called Araya in Japan (where they are probably of terminal Pleistocene age), and which also occur in the earliest horizon at Verkholenskaia Gora (12,500 B.P.).

The heavy tool tradition is reflected in a group of sites in the vicinity of Khabarovsk on the Amur, the type site being Osipovka. These sites contain a very distinctive complex which, coupled with the absence of pottery and their stratigraphic position in a yellow loam horizon, has led to their being considered as probably early Holocene in age. The big adze- or skreblo-like tools made on pebbles are associated with bifacial foliate spear points or daggers, many indistinguishable from Lerma or Cascade points of North America, or from illustrations of some of the foliate points at Ushki in Kamchatka from the 10,360 year level (fig. 2.3). Also present are Gobi cores and chipped almond-shaped axes or adzes, which occur in a wide range of sizes and evidently were used for wood working. A small-tool industry of scrapers, perforators, medial burins, and a small number of microblades completes the picture.

In Manchuria, two sites near Harbin (Ku-hsiang-t'un and Ta-kou) and the site of Djalai-nor in the extreme northwest were classified as Mesolithic by Kwang-chih Chang, apparently on the basis of typology (microblades, pressure flaking, projectile points) and presumed economy (forest hunting). They also were reported to contain elements of Pleistocene fauna. Recent investigations at Ku-hsiang-t'un have disproved the association with the fauna and established the presence of pottery. Since the lithic industry at Djalai-nor is very similar, its Mesolithic status now seems dubious. It is to be expected that Manchuria, except probably the western portion, would show its closest affinities with North China on the one hand and the Pacific coast of Siberia on the other, and stand in contrast to Siberia and Mongolia. The discovery of well-dated early Holocene sites in this region will be awaited with the greatest interest.

Figure 2.3. Points from Osipovka site, Khabarovsk (photograph by Roger Powers).

Mongolia — at least the northern half — seems to continue its cultural unity with interior Siberia — especially with Trans-Baikal. But it should be borne in mind that although a number of sites (e.g., the upper horizon at Moil'tyn-am) are typologically equated with the Siberian Epipalaeolithic and are attributed to the early Holocene, their actual age has not been established with certainty. A comparable direct transition from Epipalaeolithic to Neolithic in Mongolia seems assumed by Soviet scholars. The Mongolian Neolithic is characterized by microblades and associated small tools, with pottery. Many elements of the lithic industry seem technologically "Mesolithic," but it must be remembered that such technical traditions persisted late in Northeast Asia and commonly occur in Neolithic contexts in various places. However, an industry of this type without pottery was reported by N. C. Nelson of the Andrews expedition from Shabarakh-usu in the central Gobi in an undisturbed stratigraphic context, underlying a Neolithic occupation. The existence of such a true "Mesolithic" Shabarakh culture is accepted by the Hungarian archaeologist Gabori, who has made two recent field trips to Mongolia. On the other hand, the Soviet expeditions have also examined the site on more than one occasion, and positively assert that pottery occurs in all levels: that is, that there is no evidence of a nonceramic occupation that might be considered Mesolithic. At the present, the matter remains unresolved. At any rate, we do not know the age of these Mongolian small tool industries, although their presence in desert regions — including sand dune areas — suggests that it was likely to have been before or after the drier climatic optimum.

To summarize our survey of earlier postglacial times, the major difficulty in many areas in interpreting the limited archaeological evidence is the uncertainty as to what materials actually belong to this period of time. For the most part the attribution is typological, yet many of the elements involved were in use in the late Palaeolithic and/or persisted well into the Neolithic. Only in interior Siberia are there a few sites with faunal or stratigraphic evidence. Nor do we have any idea of the time range of industries that are sometimes viewed as "Mesolithic." On the Pacific coast of Siberia, cross-dating with the Japanese sites of known age should eventually be possible when more is known about possible shared traits.

In view of this limited available evidence, little can be said regarding human ecology or population movements in what must have been a crucial period of human history in this part of the world. The interior populations had made a successful forest adaptation. In the far northeast there were tundra-adapted populations, as evidenced by the Ushki find in Kamchatka. The Anangula site provides additional evidence of man's ability to live in the far north, and of the presence at this time (c. 8400 years ago) of a group of ultimate Asiatic origin on the shores of the Bering Sea. Various writers have stressed the wide distribution of the so-called Gobi (wedge-shaped) cores as evidence of contact between the steppe, the Pacific coast, and Alaska at this time level, but it should be borne in mind that not enough is yet known about the time horizon and typology of these artifacts to enable us to assess their historical significance. They may well have been overstressed in the literature. In connection with population history, it should be remembered that land routes no longer existed between the Asian mainland and Alaska or the Japanese islands, and that movement north of the Amur along the Pacific coast was unlikely. On the other hand, the capability of establishing at least some contact by water must have had its beginnings in postglacial times, and there is good reason to feel that Japan was by no means isolated by its surrounding waters.

The term "Neolithic" as used in Northeast Asia has no socio-economic connotations of food production and village life, but simply refers to that stage of cultural development in each area from the first appearance of pottery to the establishment of an effective metallurgy — or to the time of historic contact in the regions which did not adopt metal working. Thus, the Neolithic lasted until the Russian conquest in the far north, but ended perhaps 3600 years ago in the region of Lake Baikal. However, since metallurgy brought no significant change in life and culture in the northern forest zone — being simply grafted onto the existing pattern — the prehistory of this area down to

European contact will be treated here as a whole.[1] Evidence of Neolithic occupation is comparatively abundant and widespread in mainland Northeast Asia, although many less accessible regions are still poorly known. However, the broad outlines for the entire area are clear in most respects, and more detailed evidence is accumulating rapidly. On the other hand, our knowledge of the human population is very inadequate and relates almost entirely to the region of Lake Baikal, with a very few scattered finds elsewhere. Much hypothesizing about Neolithic population history is inevitably based on extrapolation from the historic populations, and Soviet escholars view certain modern ethnic groups such as the Yukagir and Gilyak as direct descendants of the Neolithic inhabitants of their general areas. In certain regions cultural sequences have by now been worked out, so that sites and cultures in these regions can be arranged in proper temporal relationship with more or less assurance, although differences of opinion exist in some cases. Usually these sequences serve as chronological yardsticks, being extended by typological cross-dating so that almost all of mainland Northeast Asia is served by one or another. Aside from such cross-dating, which involves certain assumptions of contact and contemporaneity, the time relationships between remains in different regions are always open to question, and will remain so until there is a very considerable increase in the number of radiocarbon dates from the area. At present, they contribute very little to Neolithic chronology, and nearly all absolute age estimates are either guesses or extrapolations from better-known (though not always well-dated) cultures of Europe and Central Asia (in the case of interior Siberia) or from the presumed but utterly baseless "chronology" that has been popular for the Chinese Neolithic (in the case of the Pacific coast). This unsatisfactory situation with regard to chronology — equalled elsewhere probably only in China — is the major stumbling block to any real understanding of human history in mainland Northeast Asia during the Neolithic stage. The estimated chronology which shapes current thinking tends to be conservative, and we may expect radical revisions and re-evaluations when it is replaced by sufficient absolute dates — judging, at any rate, from the surprising ceramic time depth now revealed in Japan, which can scarcely be an isolated phenomenon in East Asia.

Purely on the basis of archaeological evidence, the Neolithic was the time of the widespread occupation of Northern Asia by man, although we know by inference that man must have been in at least portions of the area at times previously. Population is thought to have been sparse and scattered, but archaeological sites are now numbered in the hundreds rather than in the dozens as back in the Pleistocene.

We are dealing now with conditions like the present day in terms of

1. Soviet writers feel obliged to adhere to the old "Three Ages" concept with its ideological overtones, and hence lay great stress on any evidence for the use of bronze and iron.

climate and environment. Most Neolithic remains are assumed to postdate the climatic optimum, at least those in northern regions where the change would be noticeable. The only exception at present is the multi-level Ushki site in Kamchatka, where one horizon, on pollen evidence, is considered to fall in the optimum. It is hard to believe that a closer correlation will not be demonstrated between extensive occupation of the far north and climatic amelioration.

The major cultural differences between interior Siberia and the Pacific coast continue to be apparent. The interior typically shows a development out of preceding technological patterns, the only major additions being pottery, ground stone for heavy tools (later metal), and primary dependence on the bow for hunting. There was gradual change and replacement in other items of technology. The economic pattern (hunting and fishing) and culture were simply refinements of the original forest adaptation. Major traditions can be seen spreading over large areas.

The picture in Yakutia (Lena basin) is the best documented in terms of stratigraphy and dating, based on a number of sites along the Aldan River, in particular the important and well-reported stratified site of Bel'kachi I. An early Neolithic horizon radiocarbon dated at 5970 ± 70 B.P. (LE-676) contains hand-moulded sand-tempered pottery of egg or parabaloid shape, the exterior of which is covered with net or mat impressions (fig. 2.4). This is the oldest dated pottery in Siberia — about 4920 calendar years B.C. The associated stone inventory is virtually unchanged from the preceding (early postglacial) Sumnagin culture of the general area. The overlying "developed" Neolithic (Bel'kachinsk culture) is characterized by distinctive pottery: cord-wrapped paddle impressed, manufactured by the paddle and anvil technique (figs. 2.7, 2.8). It is difficult to identify an outside source for this, which is nowhere as abundant as on the Aldan. There is much continuity from the early Neolithic in stone and bone tools, but with considerable additions seemingly borrowed from many directions. The large number of burins is particularly distinctive. This Bel'kachinsk culture is very widespread in Yakutia, and is assigned to the third millennium B.C. The late Neolithic, also widespread, is attributed to the second millennium B.C. It is characterized by equally distinctive pottery: check-stamped by beating with a grooved paddle, and often tempered with animal hair (fig. 2.11). Again, its origin is unclear. There is a sharp decrease in blade tools, blades being used almost entirely as inserts in slotted artifacts, unretouched. The majority of tools are made from flakes. It is hypothesized that this Neolithic population of Yakutia represents the ancestors of the modern Yukagir.

The Lena Neolithic is of particular interest for New World prehistory; many scattered trait analogues have been pointed out, the significance of which is unclear, and for a time it was widely hypothesized as a major source

Map 3. Mainland Northeast Asia in the Neolithic.

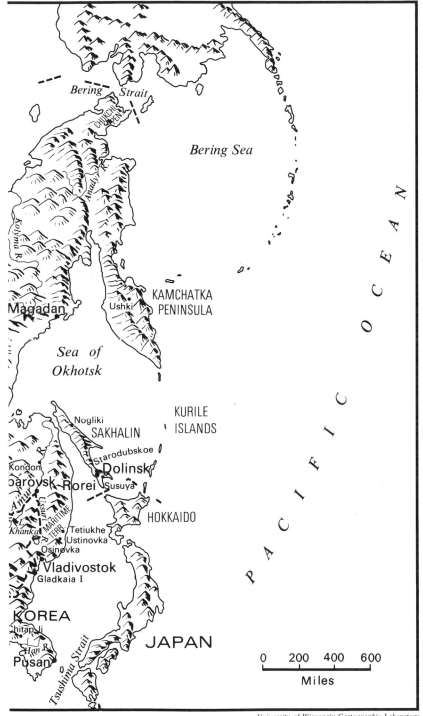

Bering Strait

CHUKCHI PEN.

Bering Sea

Anadyr R.

Kolyma R.

Magadan

Ushki

KAMCHATKA
PENINSULA

PACIFIC OCEAN

Sea of
Okhotsk

Nogliki

KURILE
ISLANDS

SAKHALIN

Starodubskoe

Kondon

Dolinsk

barovsk-Rorei

Susuya

Amur

Ussuri R.

MARITIME TERR.

Khanka

HOKKAIDO

Tetiukhe

Ustinovka

Osinovka

Vladivostok

Gladkaia I

KOREA

Chitap-li

Han R.

Pusan

Tsushima Strait

JAPAN

| 0 | 200 | 400 | 600 |

Miles

Figure 2.4. Bel'kachi I: early Neolithic pottery (after Mochanov).

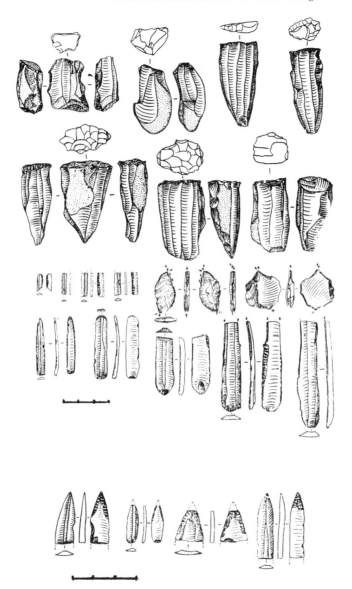

Figure 2.5. Bel'kachi I: early Neolithic cores and small tools (after Mochanov).

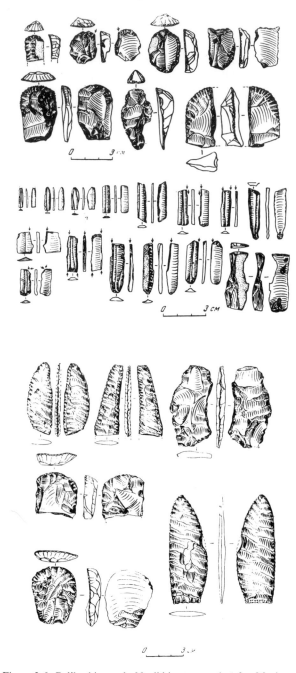

Figure 2.6. Bel'kachi I: early Neolithic stone tools (after Mochanov).

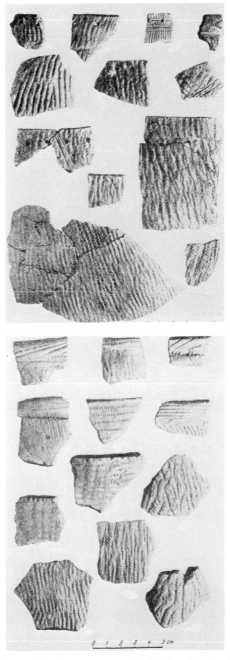

Figure 2.7. Bel'kachi I: cord-marked sherds. Bel'kachinsk culture ("developed" Neolithic) (after Mochanov).

Figure 2.8. Bel'kachi I: cord-marked vessel. Bel'kachinsk culture (after Mochanov).

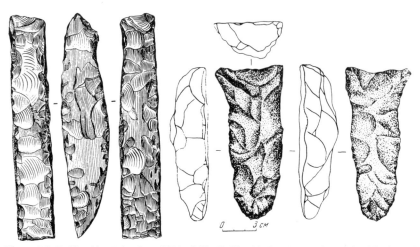

Figure 2.9. Bel'kachi I: "developed" Neolithic (Bel'kachinsk culture) adzes (after Mochanov).

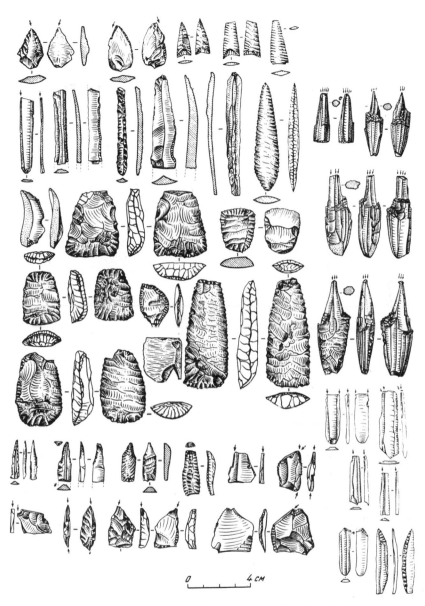

Figure 2.10. Bel'kachi I: "developed" Neolithic (Bel'kachinsk culture) small tools (after Mochanov).

Figure 2.11. Bel'kachi ɪ: late Neolithic sherds, predominantly check-stamped (after Mochanov).

for the Woodland ceramic tradition of eastern North America. The only New World pottery now generally accepted as of Asiatic origin — the Norton ceramic tradition of Alaska — seems to have been derived from the middle and late stages of the Lena basin. The Arctic Small Tool tradition, which entered Alaska early in the third millennium B.C., finds its nearest counterpart in the Bel'kachinsk culture, although it probably represents a northern tundra variant not yet pinpointed in Siberia.

In the mid-second millennium B.C. objects of copper and bronze began to appear in Yakutia, and eventually there is evidence of local bronze casting on a small scale. This was later replaced by iron. This limited use of metal brought no essential change in the culture and way of life. Finally, in the first millennium A.D. a cattle-breeding group of Turkic affinities penetrated the middle Lena valley from the Baikal region to the south, mixed with the existing population, and gave rise to the modern Yakut.

The Neolithic of the Lake Baikal region, concentrated especially along the upper Angara River, has been well known for many years. (For fuller

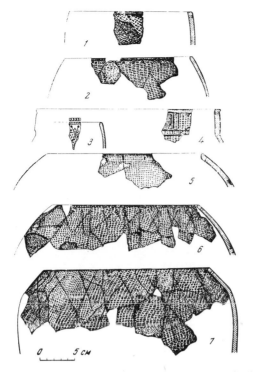

Figure 2.12. Bel'kachi ı: late Neolithic check-stamped pottery (after Mochanov).

treatment, see Michael 1958.) For this reason it often represents *the* Siberian Neolithic in the minds of foreigners, whereas it is only one of a number of regional manifestations. Despite the abundant materials recovered, the picture here is less clear than in Yakutia. There are no good dates and no relevant stratigraphy published to date, and the evidence has been interpreted in several different ways. A sequence of three stages was worked out over thirty years ago by A. P. Okladnikov on the basis of a seriation of burials in the Irkutsk area, and this still bulks large as a temporal framework for a considerable area of central Siberia. Subsequent excavation of settlement sites on the Angara River, not yet published in any detail, is claimed to confirm the sequence, although no "pure" settlements of any one stage seem to have been found. The initial Isakovo stage (fig. 2.15) is known only from a small number of burials scattered among those of other types in several cemeteries. Some of its distinctive traits (which are felt to be typologically archaic) occur elsewhere in mixed contexts where they are always taken to imply an early date for such assemblages. A purely guess date of 4000–3000 B.C. is currently given, and an entirely hunting economy is thought to be reflected in the burial equipment (though it has now been shown that fishing was already established

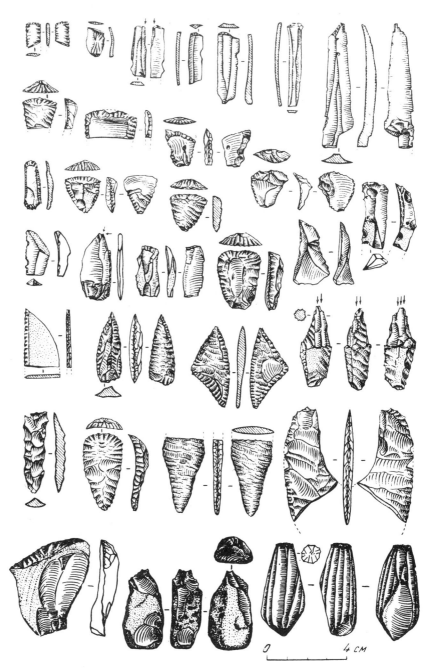

Figure 2.13. Bel'kachi I: late Neolithic small tools (after Mochanov).

here early in the Holocene at Ust'-Belaia). However, the Isakovo sample is so small that not too much weight should be attached to it. The second (Serovo) stage (figs. 2.17, 2.18) represents the "classic" period of the Baikal Neolithic; it is placed by Okladnikov at 3000–2500 B.C. although most western scholars have preferred to see it later by 500 years. In either case such figures represent no more than opinions, although they tend to be taken very seriously in the world at large. The upper and middle Angara River valley held a considerable population at this time, and Serovo cultural traits (interpreted as influence) may be seen on the Yenisei, in Trans-Baikal, and as far as Inner Mongolia (presumed migration from the Baikal hearth). The Serovo compound bow, backed with bone plates, is at present the oldest known occurrence of this type (fig. 2.23). The final (Kitoi) stage is less differentiated. It is seen as consolidating the cultural and technological gains achieved during the Serovo efflorescence and is considered transitional to the subsequent metal-using culture. Its burials are characterized by red ochre and composite fishhooks (interpreted as greater emphasis on fishing). There seems to be no distinctive pottery style, as far as can be ascertained from published sources.

Rather than reflecting "stages," these complexes might just as well represent intrusions of outside groups into an area of overlap. The prevailing concept of the Baikal area as a major cultural hearth from which influences radiated is an assumption arising from the priority of the excavations in this area. It is possible to see interior Siberia as comprising two major culture areas — Western Siberia and the Lena basin, with the Baikal region as primarily a blend of the two. Certainly the dominant ceramic influence in the Baikal area is clearly western (dentate stamping, stab and drag); other wares also have outside affinities, for example, in the Lena-Aldan area.

The appearance of small amounts of copper and bronze brought no essential change in the culture, and only minor differences in the inventory. This period, known as Glazkovo, is assigned to the eighteenth to thirteenth centuries B.C.

Trans-Baikal — the vast rugged area east of Lake Baikal as far as the Amur valley and south of the Lena basin — is still little known archaeologically. Prehistoric settlements are represented only by surface collections from the Selenga, Onon, and Chikoi river valleys. The material recovered indicates cultural links with the surrounding areas: the Lena, northern Manchuria, Mongolia, and, of course, the Baikal Neolithic. The so-called Daurian culture is regarded as the earliest known post-Palaeolithic occupation, both on typological grounds (including apparent absence of pottery) and from its stratigraphic position at the lower border of a buried soil horizon. Its actual age is, of course, completely unknown, but it exhibits strong influence from the microlithic traditions of the steppe zone. It is characterized by highly

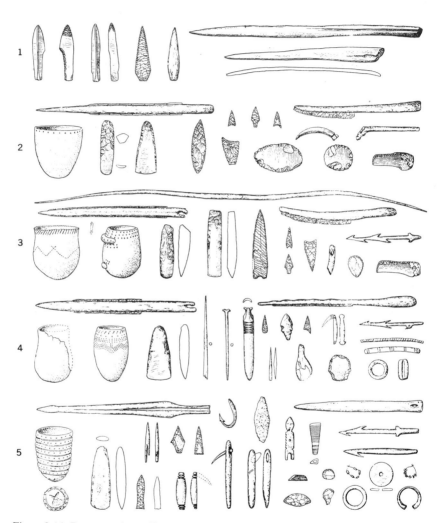

Figure 2.14. Representative artifacts of the sequence of cultural stages in the Baikal area according to Okladnikov. 1 — Khina; 2 — Isakovo; 3 — Serovo; 4 — Kitoi; 5 — Glazkovo (after Okladnikov).

Figure 2.15. Impressions of nets applied to Isakovo pottery (after Okladnikov).

developed lamellar technique, denticulate retouch, and particularly by distinctive single-shouldered arrow points (Daurian points).[2] It is thought to reflect a population of small bands of roving hunters. Later remains represent an evolved Neolithic that is seen as an extension of contemporary cultures in both the Lena and Baikal regions. Apparently the area was then marginal to these hearths of cultural development. The only habitation site to be fully excavated and described — Shilka Cave on the Amur headwaters — is very late Neolithic or early Bronze Age in cultural terms. It also yielded a cranium which more closely resembles that of modern Tungus than does any other prehistoric find and reinforces the historical deduction that this region was the original Tungus homeland.

The ecological pattern and broad cultural tradition represented by Trans-Baikal includes Mongolia and the adjacent portion of Manchuria as well. Neolithic remains in these areas are associated with an active period of soil formation, when there were forests in the river valleys and a milder and rainier

2. These latter, a form of what are generally termed blade arrowheads, are now thought to represent a borrowing from the Middle Amur, where the general category is abundant. Found from Lake Baikal to Hokkaido, they seem to constitute a widespread and short-lived horizon marker. It should be noted that G. Medvedev maintains that these artifacts were not used as projectile points, but rather as perforators of some sort.

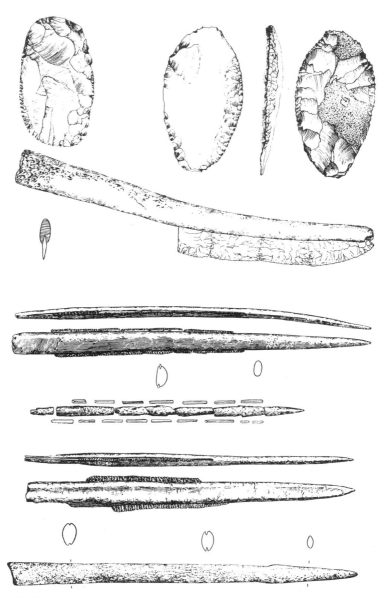

Figure 2.16. Isakovo stage: skreblo, slotted knife, and spear points with insert blades (after Okladnikov).

Figure 2.17. Serovo stage: vessel **with suspen**sion lugs (after Okladnikov).

Figure 2.18. Serovo burial with bow (after Okladnikov).

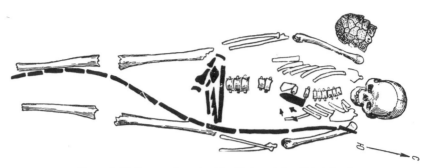

Figure 2.19. Serovo stage: burial with bow (after Okladnikov).

climate. In Mongolia, the Neolithic is known from abundant surface finds associated with present or former water-courses and lakes and typically combines a small-tool lithic industry with pottery. The only in situ remains to which reference can be found is the famous unpublished site of Shabarakh-usu, where the earliest level found by Soviet investigators is described as an Early Neolithic with Serovo-type pottery and small tools in a two-meter deposit of reddish-brown loam which was overlain by one meter of light grey buried soil, three and a half meters of sand, a Late Neolithic occupation, and more sand on top. This earliest level is identified with the nonpottery Mesolithic horizon reported by Nelson, which was discussed above. Despite the proximity of the Mongolia-Trans-Baikal area to the major center of contemporary cultural development in northern China, the historic frontier between the two different worlds of "the steppe and the sown" — later to be embodied in the Great Wall — is already clearly evident. Chinese influence is not discernible in Trans-Baikal until the Bronze Age, and even then it may represent Chinese-influenced Manchurian groups from the Jehol-Liaoning area rather than direct contact with North China itself.

The Pacific coast of Siberia (Soviet Far East), as we have pointed out, has been a completely different world from the interior from the beginnings of human history. This is nowhere more evident than in the Neolithic, with only sporadic instances of a breach of the geographic and cultural barrier — mostly, as might be expected, along the natural gateway of the Amur and its tributaries. Population movements and relationships must have continued to be channeled primarily north and south along the coast, linking up at the northern extremity with Alaska and on the south with Korea and Manchuria and, to some extent, the Japanese islands. As might be expected from the vast distances and the physiographic conditions, this coastal world may be divided into a number of culture areas: (1) the Middle Amur valley; (2) the Lower Amur; (3) the southern Maritime Territory (Vladivostok area); (4) Sakhalin; (5) the north coast of the Okhotsk Sea; (6) Kamchatka; and (7) the coasts and rivers of the Chukchi Peninsula (Chukotka). Only limited information is

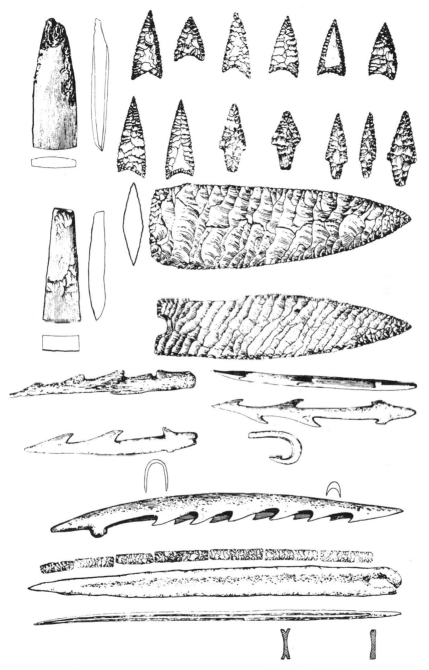

Figure 2.20. Serovo stage artifacts (not to scale) (after Okladnikov).

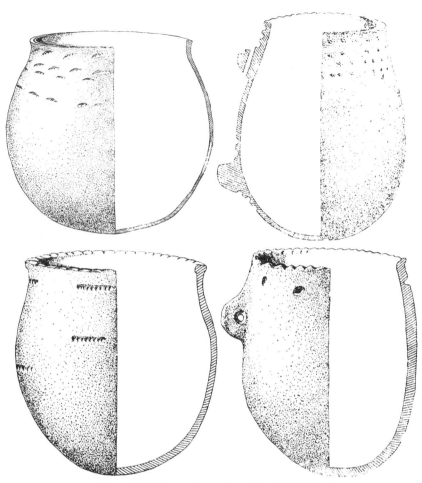

Figure 2.21. Serovo stage pottery (after Okladnikov).

Figure 2.22. Serovo stage pottery (after Okladnikov).

Figure 2.23. Bone reinforcements from Serovo compound bows (after Okladnikov).

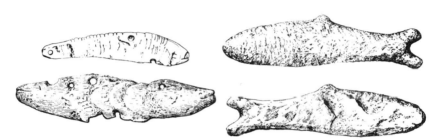

Figure 2.24. Stone fish effigies — possibly lures (after Okladnikov).

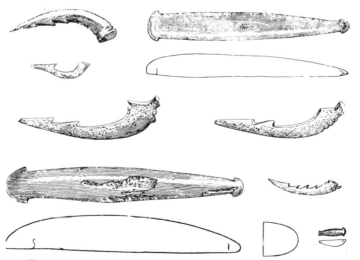

Figure 2.25. Kitoi stage: composite fishhooks (after Okladnikov).

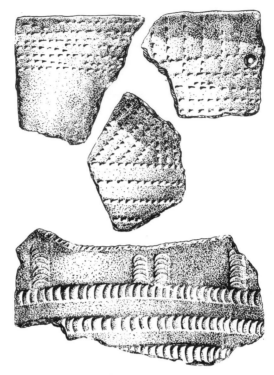

Figure 2.26. Sherds from Ulan-Khada with dentate and stab-and-drag decoration (after Oklad-nikov).

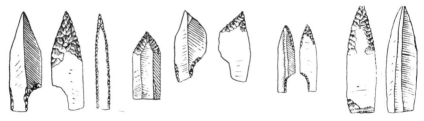

Figure 2.27. "Blade arrowheads" from Trans-Baikal (after Okladnikov).

available as yet on the Amur region: the major fieldwork has taken place only in recent years. The other areas are better known, with considerable information in English. A remarkable series of prehistoric Eskimo skeletal remains was recovered at the Uelen and Ekven sites on Bering Strait, but elsewhere only a single representative of the prehistoric population of the entire Pacific coast has been reported.

The Middle Amur area is best known from fieldwork done in 1961–65 in the vicinity of Blagoveshchensk and the tributary Zeia River valley, in the course of which more than fifty Stone Age sites were investigated. Four Neolithic cultures are currently recognized in the area, two of which (the Novopetrovka blade culture and the Gromatukha culture) are regarded as early since their lithic industries are characterized by features considered to be typologically archaic. The former, known from the sites of Konstantinovka and Novopetrovka, is a very distinctive complex. Almost all artifacts are made from lamelles, obtained from five types of cores including "epi-Levallois," "Gobi," and a type similar to Maringer's tongue-shaped Mongolian cores. Such artifacts include "blade arrowheads" and burins. There are also rectangular-section adzes and numerous net sinkers. The culture was initially classified as Mesolithic, but subsequent excavations have revealed a limited amount of flat-bottomed pottery with notched applique. Settlements are composed of rounded rectangular pit houses with (apparently) smoke hole entrances, and the economic pattern is inferred as being one of sedentary

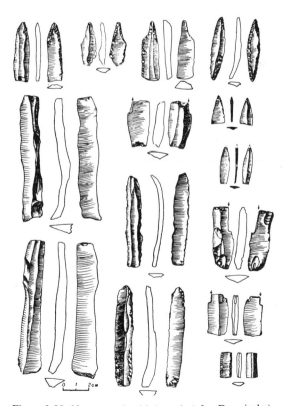

Figure 2.28. Novopetrovka: blade tools (after Derevianko).

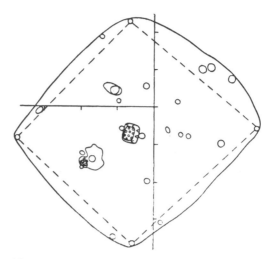

Figure 2.29. Novopetrovka: pit house (after Derevianko).

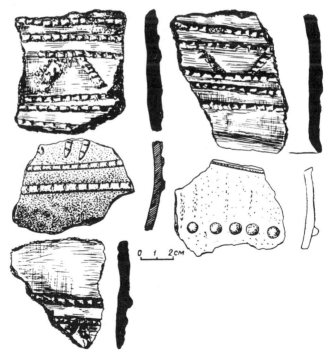

Figure 2.30. Novopetrovka: pottery (after Derevianko).

fishers and hunters. Striking similarities in lithic technology are seen with the Ustinovka workshop site on the Pacific coast, and the Novopetrovka complex is regarded as a survival of the same technological tradition. This genetic relationship, plus the fact that the Novopetrovka sites occur in a stratigraphic position suggesting that they are distinctly earlier than other Neolithic remains in the region, leads the excavator, Derevianko, to postulate considerable antiquity, but provides no basis for assigning a date. It is of interest that applique (linear relief) pottery is currently thought to be the oldest type in Japan, and that blade arrowheads are thought to be associated with the time of transition from preceramic to ceramic cultures in Hokkaido.

Equally distinctive, but quite different, is the Gromatukha culture, known from Sergeevka and sites on the Gromatukha River above Svobodnyi. The most conspicuous features of the lithic industry are the heavy unifacial flaked adzes and large side scrapers made of whole flat pebbles. Along with this there are laurel-leaf knives, tiny foliate arrowpoints with fine ''Solutrean'' retouch, and artifacts made of lamelles (though not as numerous as in the Novopetrovka culture): blade arrowheads, burins, and end scrapers. The

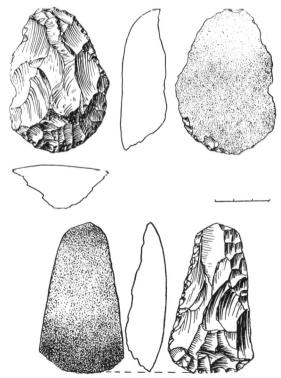

Figure 2.31. Gromatukha: adze-like tools made from pebbles (after Okladnikov).

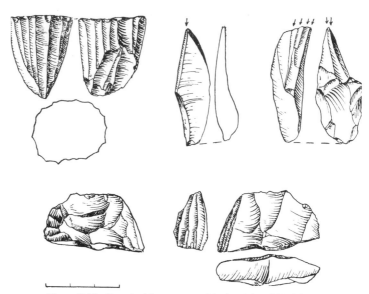

Figure 2.32. Gromatukha: cores and burins (after Okladnikov).

prismatic and conical cores from which the lamelles were produced are considerably smaller than at Novopetrovka. A number of elements suggest close
relationships with the nonceramic and supposedly early Holocene Osipovka
complex at Khabarovsk, leading Derevianko to postulate an influx of a new
population from the Lower Amur and Ussuri into the Middle Amur, and to
see Gromatukha as reflecting the last traces of the ancient pebble-based technological tradition of the late Pleistocene. Similarities are also evident in the
Manchurian Neolithic sites at Ang-ang-hsi near Tsitsihar and at Hailar.
Grafted onto this presumably indigenous lithic industry is a ceramic tradition
of alien orgin that must stem from interior Siberia to the north and west — the
Lena basin and even Lake Baikal. Vessels are decorated with impressions of a
cord-wrapped paddle, stab-and-drag, and comb-punctate. Settlements are also
quite different: there are no pit houses, only cobblestone hearths that presumably were associated with impermanent above-ground structures. The ecological pattern is thought to have been one of semi-nomadic or nomadic hunters
and fishers. Derevianko hypothesizes that all these manifestations represent a
group of related tribes who occupied the Middle Amur, northern Manchuria,
and adjacent parts of Trans-Baikal and Mongolia at around 3000 B.C. It
should be emphasized that there is no basis for assigning this or any other
date, although it seems likely that the Gromatukha culture is more recent than
the Novopetrovka.

Placed later in time with more assurance, both in terms of typology and
evidence of farming, are the settlements on Osinovoe Lake near Voikovo

and related remains. Here there are no more big unifacial tools, no blade cores or lamelles that gave the preceding cultures their ancient hue. Chipped artifacts are made from flakes struck from unprepared chalcedony nodules. Grinding slabs and milling stones, along with remains of millet, indicate farming as well as fishing — a pattern further suggested by the fact that the remains of this culture are confined to the chernozem zone of the Middle Amur. The population was sedentary, living in large pit houses similar in construction to those of the Novopetrovka culture. Their thin, polished, well-fired pottery is flat-bottomed and decorated with notched applique — again recalling their predecessors. Derevianko tends to see a genetic link. He suggests a dating of c. 2500–1800 B.C., which is in line with the conventional Neolithic chronology.

The fourth Neolithic culture on the Middle Amur is so closely similar to that of the Lower Amur that it is considered to represent a movement of population from the latter area around 1800 B.C., which by about 1500 B.C. had resulted in the settlement of considerable areas of the Amur valley. The pit houses and the pottery are like those at such Lower Amur type sites as Kondon and Suchu Island. The abundance of net sinkers (four types) confirms the expected role of fishing, but the mattocks, pestles, grinding slabs, and milling stones are taken to indicate farming as well. The dating is held down by the presumed age of the Lower Amur Neolithic and is probably underesti-

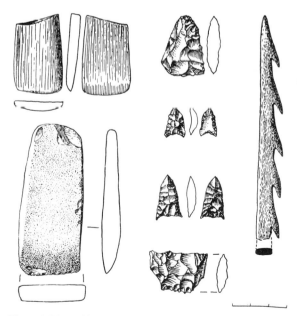

Figure 2.33. Artifacts from Osinovoe Lake (after Okladnikov).

mated. Nor is there any evident basis for placing any of these latter three Neolithic cultures relative to one another, so that the present sequence is still hypothetical.

The economic basis for the Lower Amur population was provided by the great annual fish runs, resulting in a situation comparable to that found in the Northwest Coast of North America. The pattern was one of sedentary settlements of unusually large size, with a tendency toward occupancy of the same locality over long periods of time owing to the limited number of optimal sites. This pattern is well exemplified in the group of sites near Kondon (excavated in 1961–63), which run the gamut from evolved Neolithic to medieval. The extensive Neolithic settlement consists of a group of oval or round pit houses, and considerable age was inferred from the fact that these pits, unlike later ones, are completely filled in and difficult to locate. However, the single radiocarbon date is only 4520±25 years (GIN-170) — or about 3300 calendar years B.C. Unfortunately, there is no preservation of bone in the Amur sites, which severely limits information on economic life, to say nothing of the inhabitants themselves. Of particular interest at Kondon was the find of a clay female figurine.

In 1965–66 excavations at the stratified site of Voznesenovka provided a basis for periodization of the Lower Amur Neolithic sites for the first time. The site has three stratigraphically distinct Neolithic levels overlain by Iron Age and a Mo-he occupation. The earliest level is characterized by small tools, zoned dentate pottery of truncated conical form, and another ware featuring stamped triangular designs sometimes appearing to have been executed by a cord technique, perhaps a cord-wrapped stick. Occasionally this ware has a polished bright red surface. Since the closest analogies are found at the Malyshevo site below Khabarovsk, this stage of the Neolithic has been named Malyshevo. The middle level is characterized by meander-decorated pottery and also the famous "Amur net" decoration (fig. 2.34) and has its closest analogies at Kondon. Late Neolithic pottery is decorated with vertical zigzags applied by a dentate stamp or roller, or with spiral ornament. There are also plain vessels with narrow necks. The lithic inventory includes both heavy tools made of split pebbles and slate arrowpoints and knife blades. Suchu Island is the type site, a settlement of huge pit houses up to ninety meters in circumference. A wide variety of polished axes and adzes indicate considerable wood working (and the capability of boat-building); actual evidence of fishing is limited to stone clubs assumed to have been used for dispatching large fish. The striking decorative art of the historic Amur tribes seems to have its roots in the Neolithic, as exemplified by motifs on the richly decorated pottery, rather than having arisen as a result of Chinese influence as had been generally supposed. The complex curvilinear art style is in marked contrast to the simple geometric-rectilinear style that characterizes interior

Figure 2.34 "Amur net" pottery from lower level at Pkhusun Bay (after Okladnikov).

Siberia from the Neolithic to modern times. Lower Amur pottery of indigenous type is also all flat-bottomed, unlike interior Siberia, and vessels are often large (forty to fifty centimeters high), suggesting that they were used for storage and not simply for cooking. Here as elsewhere on the Amur, weaving of plant fibers is indicated by numerous spindle whorls, some of which could also have served as loom weights.

There is substantial continuity from Neolithic to historic times in the pattern of life in the Amur valley. During the first millennium B.C. there was a rather uniform early Iron Age culture throughout the valley. Millet farming was the principal economic base on the middle Amur, and some fortified villages were built. Otherwise there was little essential change. In the first centuries A.D. the valley was occupied by the Mo-he people.

Within the Maritime Territory, despite its comparatively small size, a certain subregionalism is apparent. The northern coast is one such subregion, the coast around Vladivostok another, while the interior district around Lake Khanka and the Ussuri headwaters forms the third. Since considerable material is available in English, only an outline will be presented here. The earliest cultures are fully developed Neolithic and are currently assigned no great age in line with conventional views. No bone has been preserved at any of the sites. In the north this is represented by the lower level at the stratified Tetiukhe site, where the decorative motif on the pottery is of distinctive

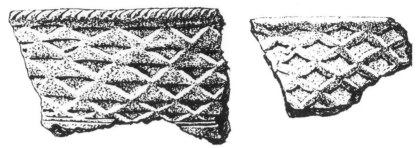

Figure 2.35. "Amur net" pottery from Tetiukhe (after Okladnikov).

Figure 2.36. Milling stone from Tetiukhe (after Okladnikov).

Lower Amur type although vessel shapes differ, indicating some influence from the Amur although not close relationship. The upper level is a settlement of twenty pit houses, some covering up to one hundred square meters. The culture is indigenous, though trade items suggest outside contacts in all directions. There are grinding slabs and milling stones, spindle whorls and textile impressions. The economy was based on hunting and fishing (nonmaritime), with grinding of some sort of food. In the south, Okladnikov sees suggestions in several localities of small wandering groups using siliceous slate for tools instead of the usual obsidian and making smooth pottery decorated with applique. He postulates this as the first Neolithic occupation. Others do not find the evidence convincing. Well established is the culture represented at Gladkaia I (or Zaisanovka I), with obsidian artifacts, a wide variety of pottery shapes and decorations, and a hunting-fishing (nonmaritime) economy with above-ground dwellings. The earliest interior site (upper level at Osinovka) shows some close parallels to Tetiukhe, while later sites differ and have closer affinities with Manchuria. The bulk of these Neolithic sites are generally assigned to the second millennium B.C., with the earliest around 2000 B.C. or very slightly earlier. Iron appears in the Vladivostok area in the eleventh to twelfth centuries B.C., coinciding with the development of the so-called Shell Mound or Sidemi culture.

Typical sites of the latter are shell middens, indicating heavy consumption

Figure 2.37. Pottery from Gladkaia I (after Okladnikov).

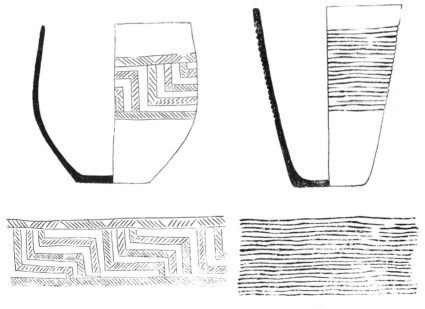

Figure 2.38. Pottery from Gladkaia I (after Okladnikov).

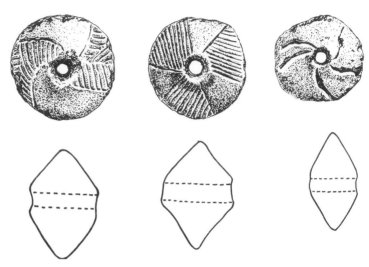

Figure 2.39. Spindle whorls from Gladkaia ı (after Okladnikov).

of shellfish at this time that seems not apparent earlier. Pigs and dogs were being bred for food, and grinding equipment was used for some sort of foodstuffs. Okladnikov believes that farming was practiced; Andreev feels the case is not proven. Okladnikov has also proclaimed the Shell Mound culture as a true maritime sea-hunting one, the first in the Soviet Far East, but his argument is convincing only with respect to fishing and certain molluscs. (It will be shown in the following chapter that Jomon Japan engaged in deep-sea fishing from earliest times.) Polished slate tools are a diagnostic of this period. Iron was limited. The population lived in large semi-subterranean houses grouped in settlements of fair size. Contemporary interior groups very likely had a farming economy. Increasingly strong Manchurian and Chinese influence seems evident from this period on. In the first millennium A.D. the southern portion of the Maritime Territory formed part of the Po-hai state and contained fortified towns.

Sakhalin is of especial interest as forming a natural bridge between Hokkaido and the Siberian mainland through which many human groups and cultural influences must have passed since well back in the Upper Pleistocene. Southern Sakhalin received a certain amount of attention from Japanese scholars prior to World War II, but there was little systematic investigation. In the past dozen years Soviet expeditions have devoted several field seasons to investigations in many parts of the island, and a number of reports have appeared. The major obstacle at the moment in the way of a better understanding of the island's prehistory is the difficulty in correlating Japanese and Soviet sites and materials: it is almost as if the two groups of investigators had

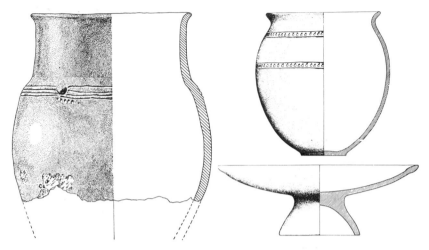

Figure 2.40. Pottery of the Shell Mound (Sidemi) culture (not to scale) (after Okladnikov).

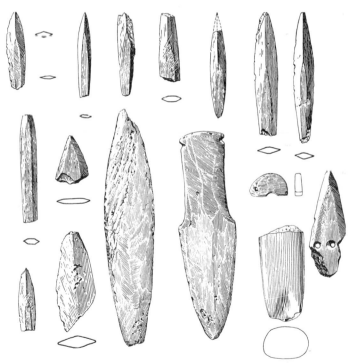

Figure 2.41. Polished slate artifacts of the Shell Mound (Sidemi) culture (scale approximate) (after Okladnikov).

worked in entirely different islands. The majority of place names have been changed by the Soviet administration, and Soviet archaeologists are either ignorant of most of the previous work or at least make no effort to identify their sites with former localities (with a very few exceptions). The oldest archaeological remains so far brought to light (in 1972) are assigned to a stage no earlier than final Mesolithic or early (preceramic) Neolithic. This complex from the Imchin site near Nogliki on the northeast coast of the island has no real counterpart elsewhere, although parallels for various elements can be seen scattered over the Soviet Far East and in Hokkaido. It is primarily a blade industry, both large blades and microblades, from conical, cylindrical, and wedge-shaped cores, and besides numerous end scrapers and burins it features tanged and rhombic arrowpoints, unifacially and bifacially worked. The excavator, R. S. Vasil'evskii, sees a significant heritage from the earlier tradition represented at Ustinovka. The pit house settlement of Nogliki I in the same area is regarded by Soviet scholars as the oldest full Neolithic site on the island, on the basis of parallels, especially in ceramics, with early sites on

Figure 2.42. Sherds from Nogliki ɪ, Sakhalin (after Kozyreva).

Figure 2.43. Vessel and sherds from Starodubskoe II, Sakhalin (after Kozyreva).

the Lower Amur and in the Maritime Territory, and on a belief that the lithic technology seems a little more "archaic" than elsewhere on Sakhalin (fig. 2.42). Next in age, in the Soviet scheme, would be the large inland pit house settlement of Starodubskoe II in the Dolinsk district of southern Sakhalin. No bone is preserved here, but a hunting-fishing-gathering economy is inferred from artifacts. The guess date of c. 1000 B.C. is supposedly based on mainland parallels which are themselves not firmly dated (fig. 2.43). Quite different cultures, and probably quite different populations, existed at this time in the north and south, with the northern population very likely an influx from the general area at the mouth of the Amur, as in historic times. The later archaeological sites — almost all in the south — are all shell middens, with bone preservation (and bone artifacts) for the first time. Also for the first time there is evidence of the appearance of a true maritime economy of sea-mammal hunters equipped with effective harpoons, including toggle types, which characterizes the area from this point on. The Susuya site, investigated by both Japanese and Soviet workers, and mercifully retaining the same name, is thought to represent the oldest stage of this new way of life. It gives the impression of the arrival of an alien group from somewhere far to the north, with a completely alien economy and the equipment to carry it on, mixing with the existing population and taking over aspects of the indigenous culture — first and foremost, the ceramic tradition. Somewhat later, when this culture blend had undergone further development, it spread down into northern Hokkaido, where it is known as the Okhotsk culture. The population involved, known from human remains at Hokkaido sites, strikes all investigators as showing definite affinity to the Arctic Mongoloids — whether Eskimoid, as some believe, or some nearer branch like the Koryak.

The long-standing mystery of the origin of these first maritime hunters of the Southern Okhotsk Sea seems now to have been solved by recent research in the Magadan area, where the Ancient Koryak culture shows striking similarities. A distinct tradition of sea-mammal hunting appears to have developed here out of an earlier shore-and-land oriented economy.

The Susuya site is dated by Soviet scholars to the last centuries B.C. and by Yoshizaki to the first few centuries A.D., and this general time range seems reasonable. Two later stages of the culture on Sakhalin are typified by the Nevel'skaia site (a few centuries later than Susuya in Soviet opinion), and Verkhniaia Sannosava and similar sites in the Rorei district which are thought to fall in the later part of the first millennium A.D. The time placement in all cases seems primarily typological. This shell midden (Okhotsk) phase on Sakhalin then came to a close, and southern Sakhalin was occupied by the Ainu population of historic times, archaeologically identified by the presence of the so-called Naiji pottery. From whence they came remains an open problem: we may guess Hokkaido. At this time the northern part of Sakhalin was presumably held, as later, by the Gilyak, whose time of arrival from the mainland is also uncertain.

It should be mentioned that a sequence of pottery wares preceding Susuya was worked out by N. Ito. Some of these wares must correspond to the earlier Soviet cultural phases, but the oldest, the Sonin linear relief ware, seems to have no counterpart in Soviet finds and may well represent the earliest known ceramic occupation of Sakhalin. It is not without interest that this type of pottery decoration seems to have appeared early on the Middle Amur as well as in Japan.

Moving north up the Pacific coast, the next prehistoric remains are encountered along the north shore of the Sea of Okhotsk, centering in the Magadan area. Here the earliest sites are shell middens containing a highly developed stone technology of traditional Neolithic type but no pottery. The people were hunters, fishers, and shellfish gatherers, living in relatively permanent settlements, but were definitely not sea hunters. Maritime culture had not yet appeared. The later sites in the area — presumably separated by a considerable hiatus in time — are considered to be without doubt the ancestors of the Koryak, practicing a true sea-hunting economy (90 percent of the food remains are sea-mammal bones). Cultural parallels are discerned with the Bering Sea on the one hand and the maritime sites of Sakhalin on the other.

Some of the most significant recent developments in the study of human prehistory in Northeast Asia have been at the outermost margin — in Kamchatka and the Chukchi Peninsula (Chutkotka). The preliminary reports are mostly readily available in English. In the opinion of the most active current investigator, N. N. Dikov, a preceramic Neolithic stage prevailed throughout the area at the general time of the climatic optimum, characterized by a core-and-blade technology with burins. This was succeeded — perhaps in roughly the second millennium B.C. — by a fully developed Neolithic with pottery and heavy ground stone tools. At this time a marked regionalism began to develop: in Kamchatka there was a distinctive culture with local peculiarities including labrets, large pit houses, and other items reminiscent of the Aleutians. During the ensuing Late Neolithic — approximately the first

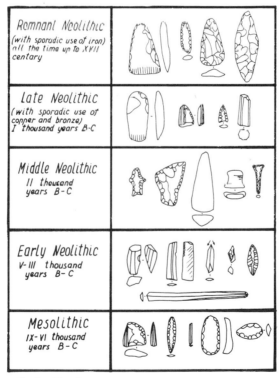

Figure 2.44. Generalized artifact inventories from the prehistoric cultural stages of Kamchatka according to Dikov.

millennium B.C. — economic differentiation was also apparent, with emphasis on fishing in Kamchatka (where the population is presumed to represent the ancestral Kamchadal) and on reindeer hunting in Chukotka (presumably the ancestral Chukchi-Koryak). The burials at Ust'-Belaia on the Anadyr, one of which is reported to have yielded a radiocarbon date equal to about 1100 calendar years B.C., belong here. The one cranium which has been described resembles that of a modern Reindeer Chukchi. At this riverine location, the economy included fish and seals as well as reindeer.

A final "Relict Neolithic" in post-A.D. times reveals five economic-cultural areas corresponding to historic ethnic groups: the Eskimo on the coast of Chukotka; an inland population (perhaps an intruding wedge of Yukagir) on the Anadyr and Main Rivers; the Koryak area (sea hunting on the coast, reindeer hunting in the interior); the Kamchadal fishing economy of central Kamchatka; and the Kurile Ainu in the southern tip of Kamchatka and the Kurile Islands, replacing the Okhotsk culture in this island chain and carrying on their maritime economy. Dikov suggests that this steady regional and local differentiation throughout several millennia reflects the corresponding processes of ethnic differentiation. Perhaps we may see in this an original roughly homogeneous Arctic Mongoloid population differentiating through time into separate linguistic and genetic groupings, with the Eskimo at one extreme and the Kamchadal at the other.

The broad ecological picture in Neolithic Siberia is one of a basic generalized hunting-fishing economy everywhere, with economic specialization developing later in only certain regions: fishing on the Amur and in Kamchatka, farming in areas adjacent to Manchuria, sea-mammal hunting on the coasts of Chukotka and the north shore of the Sea of Okhotsk, with a still later extension to Sakhalin. The limited extent and late date of maritime economy in Siberia is of particular interest, as is the concurrent indication of shifts in patterns of exploitation of a given area by man under aboriginal conditions. It is evident, for instance, that people can live by the sea without being inspired to make any use of it.

The Korean peninsula reflects a situation remarkably like that of the Near East, India, or China not so many years ago: namely, an historically important region, accessible and well-known, but one whose prehistory was a virtual blank due largely to preoccupation with spectacular remains of the historic periods. As a corollary, there was a common assumption of no great time depth. The first stratigraphically based sequence of Neolithic periods was only worked out in the last decade and partially dated by radiocarbon — unfortunately in an area (Pusan) that may have been marginal to the mainstream of cultural development. Elsewhere in the south the Neolithic is known very inadequately, from a few scattered undated sites and some study of trait distributions. The picture with regard to the later (metal) period is no better. In North Korea a great deal of salvage archaeology has been carried out in recent years (as in China), but this mass of material is only beginning to be analyzed and little has been reported as yet. Until the evidence is more fully presented, we can do little more than relay the current opinions of the archaeologists involved. Relative chronology here is based mainly on suggested developmental sequences of pottery and house types, or presence-or-absence seriation of sites. As yet there are no clearly stratified Neolithic sites: the few instances of clear stratigraphy involve Palaeolithic under Neolithic, or metal period overlying Neolithic. A current scheme in North Korea proposes an Early Neolithic, Developed Neolithic A and B stages, and a Late Neolithic — all differentiated by minor details in technical traits.

Even this limited evidence shows the outlines of a distinct regionalism. It is evident that prehistoric Korea is a geographical expression; as a unit it has no historical reality. Various regions were largely isolated from one another and often in closer contact with areas outside the peninsula. The northeast formed part of the Vladivostok (southern Maritime Territory) culture area, the northwest had close links with Manchuria, and the central portion of the peninsula (including the Han River valley) constituted a distinct culture area extending at least at times from coast to coast despite the intervening mountain barrier. The Pusan area, again, has its own character and shows evidence of at least some contact with Japan over a considerable span of time. The southwest, potentially the key area for elucidating the history of food production in Korea, is archaeologically unknown.

From its geographical situation, there has always been a tendency to view the Korean peninsula as a bridge between the two great hearths of cultural development in northeast Asia — China and Japan. Yet all evidence down at least to the Christian era suggests quite the opposite: the role of Korea in human prehistory was primarily as a barrier, not a link, between the two. This raises some interesting problems. We may wonder whether the rugged topography of the peninsula, especially in the north, was primarily responsible, or whether there was actual cultural resistance to outside influence, as seems to have been the case in contemporary Japan.

As noted above, the best sequence of Neolithic cultural development is from an area that may be marginal to the mainstream. Excavations in 1963 by the University of Wisconsin at the Tongsamdong site near Pusan revealed a stratigraphic sequence of five stages. The oldest period of occupation, labeled Chodo, is as yet undated but would seem to be contemporary with some parts of the Early Jomon of Japan. The second period (Mokto) is radiocarbon dated at about 4800 calendar years B.C. (5890 ± 140 B.P.: GX-0378). Inasmuch as the Chodo pottery is already well developed, plus the fact that there is no reason to assume that the site spans the entire Neolithic occupation of the region, it is likely that still earlier periods exist. At the very least, a considerable time depth must now be allowed for the beginnings of the Neolithic in the Korean peninsula — far in excess of anything hitherto allotted, but certainly in no way surprising in view of the very early dates now known for ceramic origins in nearby Japan.

The economic basis at Pusan during Chodo times seems to have been both land hunting and fishing, with some gathering of shellfish. The presence of Early Jomon Sobata trade sherds indicates that contacts with Japan were already occurring, and hence that watercraft capable of negotiating the Tsushima Straights must have been in use. In the ensuing Mokto period there is abundant evidence of fishing, as well as remains of whale and sea lion. An emphasis on deep-water molluscs is seen in the next (Pusan) period, dated at about 3740 calendar years B.C. (4945±125 B.P.: GX-0379). Throughout these earlier periods there is an evolution and continuity of various ceramic traits culminating in the well-known "comb-pattern" wares which characterize the Tudo period (fig. 2.45). These wares are widespread in Korea and thus provide a potentially valuable horizon marker for correlating Neolithic developments elsewhere in the peninsula. Unfortunately, the Tudo period at Pusan is not yet satisfactorily dated. It had long been hypothesized that these "comb-pattern" wares represented an intrusion from northern Asia, and the evidence of indigenous development indicated at Tongsamdong is thus of the greatest importance. Contact with Japan is evidenced by obsidian considered to be of Japanese origin, and by the abundance of glycemeris shell bracelets, which were popular in the Late to Final Jomon of western Japan. Of particular interest are the possible indications of some limited cultivation. These include the sudden appearance of grinding equipment and of artifacts classified as stone hoes. The large size of pottery vessels also suggests food storage. Since the Pusan area is not particularly well suited to farming, but rich in marine resources, it might be expected that it would lag behind other regions of the peninsula, such as the southwest, in making major shifts in the basic economic pattern. Any cultivation introduced could well have played only a subsidiary role for some time. But the comb-ware horizon elsewhere might equally well herald important economic developments. Comb-ware sites in western Korea typically include grinding equipment and/or probable cultivating implements; one (Chitap-li) yielded carbonized grain identified as millet. (This site is assigned by the North Korean archaeologists to their Developed Neolithic A stage.) However, hunting is still in evidence. Pit houses are characteristic of such settlements.

The subsequent appearance of a limited number of bronze and iron artifacts in Korea brought no essential change. There is no good evidence of a local bronze industry in the peninsula preceding iron, although the need for a true "Bronze Age" as an evolutionary stage in Korean prehistory is strongly felt in North Korea, and efforts are made by North Korean archaeologists to

Figure 2.45. "Comb-pattern" sherds from Tongsamdong site, Pusan, Korea. Tudo period (courtesy of L. L. Sample).

demonstrate it. The only distinctive feature of this time horizon is the sudden appearance from some outside source of "megalithic" burial practices symbolized by dolmens, of which between two and three thousand exist, widely distributed. A little later, iron metallurgy became well established, coinciding with the first good evidence of rice agriculture. Here, as in Japan, the two seem to go hand in hand.

In contrast to isolated Korea, Manchuria is a crossroads, an area of cultural overlap open to impinging influences from the Pacific coast to the east, the Siberian taiga to the north, the Mongolian steppe to the west, and the farming population of China to the south.

Although as noted no indubitable preceramic sites are known, the basic cultural pattern and technology, widespread over the entire area, must have deep local roots and reflects a hunting-gathering way of life. The earlier sites

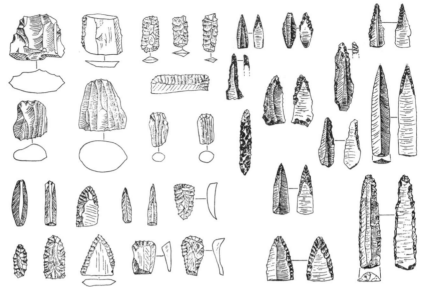

Figure 2.46. Cores and tools from Ang-ang-hsi (after Larichev).

all seem to be correlated with a black soil horizon that may represent an ancient forest cover intervening between the semi-arid loess of the terminal Pleistocene and the recent and also semi-arid soils. This basic cultural picture was subjected to increasing influence from the Neolithic of North China, beginning in Yangshao times, which probably involved the introduction of farming at an early stage in this process. Naturally, this influence was strongest in the south, and only later and in lesser degree affected the north and marginal areas.

Unfortunately our picture of prehistoric Manchuria is based primarily on surveys and sampling of sites, only a very few of which have been investigated at all extensively. In situ association of specific finds is not always certain. Relative dating depends mainly on parallels with surrounding areas, and especially on the degree and nature of Chinese influence. Attempts at broad chronological schemes are tentative and not always convincing. For example, W. C. Pei has distinguished an Early Neolithic which he calls the Lung-chiang stage, characterized by a small-tool lithic industry, pottery, and a hunting economy; and a Middle Neolithic (Lin-hsi) stage with ground stone artifacts added, some of which may be farming tools. However, since the major site of the early stage (Ang-ang-hsi) lies well to the north, it could well be more or less contemporary with the more southerly Lin-hsi sites which expectably were the first to be subjected to influences from the Chinese farming world. Within local areas, valid time differences can certainly be inferred between sites on this sort of basis, and later remains can often be cross-dated with the developing stages of Chinese civilization through shared traits or trade items. However, the overall picture can only be traced in broad outline as yet.

The indigenous Manchurian Neolithic is best reflected in the group of occupation sites near Ang-ang-hsi. Along with abundant animal, fish, and mollusc remains was a lithic small-tool industry having close analogies with Novopetrovka on the Middle Amur (core types, lamelles, blade arrowheads) and Gromatukha (bifacial foliate arrowpoints and laurel-leaf spear points or daggers). Linear relief (applique) pottery in at least one site points in the same direction. The burials at Ang-ang-hsi seem to reflect a different occupation or time period, probably later. Ceramics from these are related to wares in the southern Maritime Territory and North Korea.

Elsewhere in Manchuria, sites show varying degrees of Chinese influence on this basic pattern, from the Lin-hsi sites where it is limited mainly to probable farming tools to the mixed cultures of the lower Liao in the south with strong admixture from both Yangshao and Lungshan sources. Intermediate are the sites in the Ch'ih-feng area (such as Hung-shan-hou), where the indigenous small-tool industry and pottery of Maritime-North Korean type is associated with Yangshao pottery and farming.

The same general picture persists into the metal ages, with increasing and spreading Chinese influence in the regions suitable for farming, and the rise of pastoralism in the steppe zone of the west, closely linked with developments in Mongolia.

Bibliography

Arutiunov, S., and Sergeev, D.
    1968. "Two Millennia of Cultural Evolution of Bering Sea Hunters."
        Arctic Anthropology 5, no. 1: 72–75.
Chang, Kwang-chih
    1961. "Neolithic Cultures of the Sungari Valley, Manchuria."
        Southwestern Journal of Anthropology 17: 56–74.
Chard, Chester S.
    1961. "Time Depth and Culture Process in Maritime Northeast Asia."
        Asian Perspectives 5, no. 2: 213–16.
Derevianko, A. P.
    1969. "The Novopetrovka Blade Culture on the Middle Amur." *Arctic
        Anthropology* 6, no. 1: 119–27.
    1970. *Novopetrovskaia kul'tura Srednego Amura* [The Novopetrovka Culture of the Middle Amur]. Novosibirsk: Nauka, Sibirskoe Otdelenie.
Dikov, N. N.
    1965. "The Stone Age of Kamchatka and the Chukchi Peninsula in the
        Light of New Archaeological Data." *Arctic Anthropology* 3, no. 1:
        10–25.

Istoriia Sibiri [History of Siberia].
    1968. Vol. 1. Leningrad: Nauka.
Khlobystin, L. P.
    1969. "The Stratified Settlement of Ulan-Khada on Lake Baikal." *Arctic Anthropology* 6, no. 1: 88–94.
Medvedev, G. I.
    1969. "Results of the Investigation of the Mesolithic in the Stratified Settlement of Ust'-Belaia." *Arctic Anthropology* 6, no. 1: 61–73.
Michael, Henry N.
    1958. "The Neolithic Age in Eastern Siberia." *Transactions, American Philosophical Society* 48, pt. 2.
    1964. *The Archaeology and Geomorphology of Northern Asia: Selected Works.* Toronto: University of Toronto Press.
Mochanov, IU. A.
    1969a. *Mnogosloinaia stoianka Bel'kachi I i periodizatsiia kamennogo veka IAkutii* [The Stratified Site of Bel'kachi I and the Periodization of the Stone Age of Yakutia]. Moscow: Nauka.
    1969b. "The Early Neolithic of the Aldan." *Arctic Anthropology* 6, no. 1: 95–103.
    1969c. "The Bel'kachinsk Neolithic Culture on the Aldan." Ibid, pp. 104–14.
    1969d. "The Ymyiakhtakh Late Neolithic Culture." Ibid, pp. 115–18.
Okladnikov, A. P.
    1964. "Ancient Population of Siberia and Its Culture." In *The Peoples of Siberia*, edited by M. G. Levin and L. P. Potapov, pp. 13–98. Chicago: University of Chicago Press.
    1965. *The Soviet Far East in Antiquity.* Toronto: University of Toronto Press.
    1970. *Yakutia.* Montreal: McGill-Queen's University Press.
Sample, L. L.
    1974. *Tongsamdong: a Contribution to Korean Neolithic Culture History.* Arctic Anthropology 11, no. 2.
Tolstoy, Paul
    1958. "The Archaeology of the Lena Basin and Its New World Relationships." *American Antiquity* 23: 397–418, 24: 63–81.
Vasil'evskii, R. S.
    1969. "The Origin of the Ancient Koryak Culture on the Northern Okhotsk Coast." *Arctic Anthropology* 6, no. 1: 150–64.
Yoshizaki, Masakazu
    1963. "Prehistoric Culture in Southern Sakhalin." *Arctic Anthropology* 1, no. 2: 131–58.

3 Jomon Japan

Ten thousand years ago a cooler climate still prevailed in Japan — as shown by the fact that the temperate mixed forest extended much farther south than it does today and covered most of western Japan. Sea level was forty meters lower than the present level, so that much more coastal lowland was available for use. If the population of the time already had the littoral orientation so evident subsequently, most of the human record may be submerged. The sea rose rapidly, reaching a level five meters above the present between 7000 and 6000 years ago (the Jomon transgression), with suggestions of a climate somewhat warmer than today's. By then the existing vegetation pattern must have been established, with its two main environmental zones of eastern (temperate forest) and western (subtropical forest) Japan, plus boreal northeastern Hokkaido.

This period of change coincides with the formative stages of the Jomon cultural tradition, a pattern of life basically rooted in the temperate mixed forest environment.

Jomon Japan is one of the most abundantly documented and extensively studied areas and periods anywhere in the world. We hear estimates on the order of 75,000 sites; a bibliography on the subject published back in 1955 already listed 3869 references. However, this mass of evidence is not evenly distributed in time and space, with the result that we have inadequate knowledge of some regions and some stages. It also reflects a tremendous overemphasis on pottery typology: the bulk of the published or available evidence relates to this aspect, with relatively little information on other branches of technology or on ecology, settlement patterns, and so forth. In fairness, we should record that more interest is now developing in the broader picture of human activities, but pottery typology still dominates the scene.

Chronologically, on the other hand, the picture is unusually bright. In fact there is nothing comparable in Asia outside of the Near East. We have a good relative sequence worked out by stratigraphy in several areas and extended, perhaps overconfidently in some cases, to the rest of Japan by typological comparison of pottery wares: a sequence that has now been bolstered and given time depth by a growing number of highly consistent radiocarbon dates. The major remaining chronological gap is the absence of anything approach-

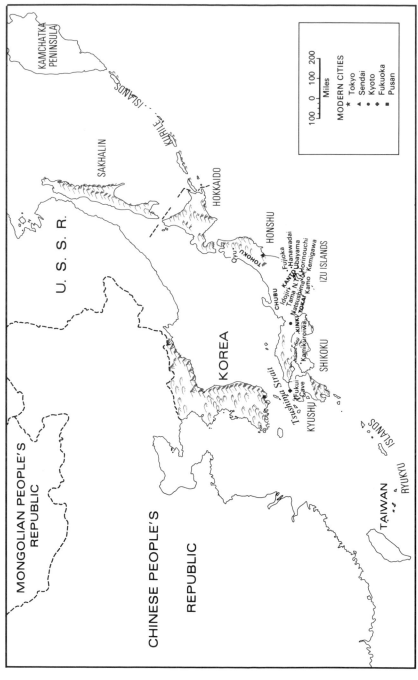

Map 4. Jomon Japan.

ing this time scale on the adjacent continent, thus making it very difficult to study relationships with the rest of Eurasia.

Geography continued to be the major single factor in the prehistory of Japan, in two ways. First, during Jomon times cultural development took place in relative isolation. Except for Hokkaido, which never seems to have completely lost touch with the mainland, outside contact depended on maritime skills and does not seem to have been extensive. Second, geography also fostered another major characteristic of the cultural picture: the marked regionalism within a relatively small area. In the Japanese islands, the habitable regions are typically separated by a rugged topography that promotes a degree of internal isolation, producing a pattern that one would not find, for example, on the North China plain. From the very start of Jomon times local pottery traditions in each region suggest the existence of separate tribal or ethnic groupings. And the basic differences in all aspects of culture between eastern and western Japan create an overall pattern in the archaeological record that persists throughout. Since the major regional differences correspond in a general way to environmental zones, it is likely that they reflect ecological adjustments emphasizing exploitation of differing economic resources.

Until recently, there appeared to be a hiatus between what were considered to be the latest manifestations of Pleistocene culture in Japan (assemblages characterized primarily by projectile points or by microblades) and the Initial Jomon culture as seen in southern Kanto (characterized by cord-wrapped-stick rolled impressed pottery [*yoriito-mon*] [fig. 3.1] and a very different assemblage of stone tools). Now, with the discovery of still older ceramic wares dating to the closing millennia of the Pleistocene and associated with microlithic or point industries of preceramic type, the typological discontinuity between preceramic and ceramic cultural manifestations no longer seems as abrupt. Further indication of possible technological continuity is provided by increasing instances in preceramic sites of stone artifacts showing evidence of working by techniques of grinding and abrasion — an achievement heretofore accorded only to the bearers of the Jomon tradition in conformance with traditional views of the history of human technology. The obvious employment of these techniques in the late Pleistocene elsewhere in the world, at least on bone, destroys the rationale for such dogma, which still shapes most thinking. To say that the hiatus no longer looms so large, however, is not to say that cultural continuity to the Jomon tradition has been demonstrated.

The initial appearance of pottery itself in Japan, on the other hand, does seem an abrupt phenomenon. The current candidate for the earliest ware — the linear relief pottery of Level III in Fukui Cave, Kyushu (fig. 3.2) — is radiocarbon dated at $12,700 \pm 500$ years (GaK-950), which is consistent with

Figure 3.1. *Yoriito-mon* pottery from Natsushima (courtesy of S. Sugihara).

other evidence. Some scholars find it difficult to believe that this represents the first attempt at ceramics, thus suggesting the introduction of ceramic technology from somewhere outside of Japan, where it had already undergone considerable development. This of course implies a very considerable time depth for ceramics somewhere in mainland East Asia. Just where this hearth might have been located is another matter. It would seem improbable that any examples of linear relief now known from the mainland could be of sufficient age to play any role in Japanese ceramic origins. Other scholars regard this oldest ware as sufficiently primitive to actually represent the beginnings of pottery, and would see Japan as one of the hearths of the independent invention of this art. The argument hinges to some extent on the interpretation of the associated microblade technology in Fukui Level III: some consider it an intrusion from the mainland, others a product of evolution from local antecedents.

Another problem is whether the other examples of very early pottery in Japan all derive from this presumed introduction (or invention), or whether the process may have been repeated, and not necessarily from the same source. Present evidence indicates that the other known occurrences are somewhat later in time. A slightly different type of linear relief has been found in the lowest level at Kamikuroiwa Rock Shelter on Shikoku, where it

Figure 3.2. Linear relief pottery from Fukui Cave (after Serizawa, by permission).

is dated at $12,165 \pm 600$ (I-944) years, but a rather different ware, the so-called fingernail-impressed (*tsumegata-mon*), is also present at this general time horizon in several localities (fig. 3.3). The historical and technological relationship of these two wares is not clear. Although the label "Incipient Jomon" has been proposed for the cultural stage reflected in these early pottery sites with their "preceramic" lithic technology, any relationship between them and the succeeding Jomon tradition is hypothetical at the moment and represents still another major problem. Evidence from this stage is as yet

Figure 3.3. *Tsumegata-mon* pottery from Hashidate (after Serizawa et al.).

too scanty to provide any deductions as to ecology, life, culture, or the historical processes that were taking place at what was obviously one of the most crucial periods of Japanese prehistory. The few sites are all inland, and mostly in caves, suggesting an interior orientation; but the main drama might have been played in the coastal zone now submerged beneath the sea.

It should be mentioned, parenthetically, that Hokkaido was isolated from the rest of Japan at this time and continued on its own path of cultural development. The first appearance of pottery on the island seems to have been 5000 years later.

The eight thousand or so years between the stage of the earliest ceramic sites in the Japanese Islands and the introduction of rice farming is occupied by the long development of the tradition and pattern of life referred to as Jomon, a name taken from a distinctive technique of pottery decoration made by means of impressions of twisted cords (fig. 3.4) which is widely characteristic. This period fits the North Eurasian definition of "Neolithic," in the sense of being a time of hunting-fishing-gathering cultures possessing pottery and before the appearance of metal. In western Japan, where the shift to rice farming first took place, the Jomon period came to an end about 400 B.C.; elsewhere, where the transformation was slower to come about, it persisted longer. And the same general pattern of life — enriched by trade goods, it is true — lingered in Hokkaido until a few hundred years ago.

The formation of the historic Japanese people and their culture begins with the succeeding Yayoi period, which saw the introduction of intensive agriculture, a new ceramic tradition (from which the period takes its name), metal, and possibly the major genetic component of the modern Japanese population, along with their language. Jomon is aboriginal, and the extent of its contribution to historic Japan — genetically, culturally, linguistically — remains probably *the* main problem of Japanese prehistory. As a working hypothesis, it is suggested that this contribution was perhaps comparable to that of the Mesolithic population of Europe to the succeeding farming cultures and peoples of the European Neolithic — a contribution likewise uncertain but suspected to be considerable. In the case of Europe, the continual invasions and reshufflings of population beginning in the late Neolithic effectively diluted any Mesolithic heritage in the subsequent stages of European history, except in the northern regions beyond the limits of effective agriculture. Japan, however, was sealed off from such interference with normal cultural processes, so that the Jomon contribution may be presumed to be a more direct and more significant factor in historic Japan. Again, the role of the far north (in this case Hokkaido) as the last refuge of aboriginal culture parallels the picture in Europe.

A span of history on the order of 8000 years documented by such an abundance of archaeological materials obviously requires subdivision into periods or cultural stages. A scheme of five stages (Initial, Early, Middle,

Figure 3.4. Examples of impressions produced by rolling twisted cords of various types (photographs by Peter Bleed).

Late, and Final Jomon), originally formulated on the basis of supposed wide-spread and conspicuous changes in pottery technology but now a more arbi-trary classification sanctified by usage, is widely accepted and will be followed here. The time placement of these stages, based on available radiocarbon dates, is shown in the accompanying table (Table 2). There is an evident time lag in the age of sites in areas more marginal to the main centers of develop-ment, and as a result there is some degree of overlap in the time spans of the five stages.

Table 2. Tentative Chronology of Japanese Prehistory

Period	Date
Preceramic	?–c. 11,000 B.C.
Early ceramic sites ("Incipient Jomon")	c. 11,000 B.C.–c. 7500 B.C.
Initial Jomon	c. 7500 B.C.–c. 5300 B.C.
Early Jomon	c. 5300 B.C.–c. 3600 B.C.
Middle Jomon	c. 3600 B.C.–c. 2500 B.C.
Late Jomon	c. 2500 B.C.–c. 1000 B.C.
Final Jomon	c. 1000 B.C.–c. 400 B.C.
Yayoi	c. 400 B.C.–c. 400 A.D.

Note: This table is based on currently available radiocarbon dates. The two oldest dates are in radiocarbon years; the remainder are in calendar years.

The origins of the Jomon tradition are still obscure. The first manifestation of some of the basic features, on present knowledge, occurs with the cord-wrapped-stick rolled (*yoriito-mon*) pottery at the famous Natsushima site near the mouth of Tokyo Bay at least 9450 years ago. In the latter part of the Initial Jomon stage the tradition was well under way in the mixed-forest zone which was to be its nuclear area throughout its existence. The basic ecological adaptation had been worked out and subsistence patterns, techniques, and equipment devised that were to persist unchanged until the end of Jomon times. These patterns were based on the rich food resources of the temperate zone, utilizing the forest but in particular the sea coast and the sea itself. So nice was the adaptation that any radical change was inhibited for many thousands of years, a situation somewhat reminiscent of the Archaic of east-ern North America and the "Neolithic" of Northern Eurasia, though in the latter case the environment, and hence the economic pattern, differed significantly, and a shift to farming under aboriginal conditions was ruled out by climate. In particular, the topography of Japan fosters coastal life and an extensive use of littoral resources not available to most of the population of Northern Eurasia. These resources, moreover, are unusually abundant around the Japanese Islands due to such factors as ocean currents. It has been hypothesized that as the coastal plains were inundated around the end of the Pleistocene the population would have turned more to the resources offered by

Figure 3.5. Typical Jomon stone tool kit from Natsushima (courtesy of S. Sugihara).

the sea. Archaeological evidence from the very beginning of Initial Jomon would seem to bear this out.[1] Subsequent transgression by higher sea levels during the Holocene would have intensified this process by creating large areas of shallow estuaries favorable for molluscs. The Jomon way of life seems to have been characterized by ample food supply but limited surplus, and was to prove resistant to the shift to a farming economy — perhaps until its economic base at length gave out. The Jomon nuclear area was marginal to any influences from outside of Japan which might occasionally affect more accessible regions such as Hokkaido or Kyushu. This maximum isolation evidently fostered conservatism and stability in cultural life.

The later Initial Jomon stage also saw the establishment of the ceramic technology which was to characterize the entire subsequent tradition, as well as the lithic complex (fig. 3.5). If the origins and process of formation of these diagnostic technologies were known, we would be a long way towards an

1. In particular, the lowest levels at Natsushima. Here the oldest cord-rolled pottery, the Igusa type, is found underneath the shell midden but not associated with marine food remains. The overlying lowest shell layer contains the dated Natsushima type pottery with fish bones as well as numerous bird and animal remains. This suggests a move to coastal areas followed by gradual establishment of a coastal economy.

understanding of the beginnings of the Jomon tradition which was to play such a major role in Japanese prehistory. At the present we can only say that no source outside of Japan is apparent. On the other hand, if its roots go back to earlier cultural complexes in Japan itself, the formative process is still unexplained.

Once established in its nuclear area, the Jomon tradition throughout its long subsequent history shows only very rare and trifling instances of seemingly alien elements suggesting possible outside influence or borrowing. Either the isolation of Japan in Jomon times was virtually complete, or else such contact as did occur exerted little effect and led only to highly selective borrowing, if any. In any case, Jomon Japan provides an ideal laboratory case study for the anthropologist of cultural development in a "closed system" — a "test tube" situation which it would be hard to duplicate elsewhere. At the same time it forces us to recognize the Japanese Islands as a cultural hearth in their own right and not as a mere passive recipient of benefits and stimuli originating elsewhere.

Such isolation during Jomon times is all the more remarkable in view of the proximity of what is assumed to have been a major and dynamic hearth of cultural development in China, whose influence at least in the later millennia spread far and wide and played a significant role in the human history of this part of the world. It might be expected that this influence would have been greatest and this role most significant in such an adjacent area as Japan. So paradoxical a situation merits attention from the student of culture history and cultural dynamics, and calls for explanation. The most obvious factor is, of course, the geographical isolation of Japan by water. Yet the water barriers involved are far less forbidding than in the case of Taiwan, which was readily reached by Lungshanoid colonists. From Pusan in Korea one can, for example, see the island of Tsushima and from the latter glimpse Kyushu. Evidence of deepwater fishing at the Natsushima site indicates that at least some coastal groups in Japan must have had adequate watercraft over 9000 years ago, and a late Initial Jomon site on one of the Izu Islands is even more convincing evidence of maritime capabilities, probably at least as early as 7500 years before the present. By around 6500 B.P. there is clear evidence of occasional trade between Kyushu and the Pusan area of Korea. Obviously, then, Japan was not completely cut off from the outside world.

At the same time, the absence of any significant alien influence on the Jomon tradition for the many thousands of years after its establishment suggests strong cultural resistance to such contacts as did occur. And the ecological context, for another thing, seems to have offered no foothold to any radically new economic pattern until the fourth century B.C., although we might expect awareness of such patterns prior to that time among at least some seagoing persons in westernmost Japan. Whatever the actual situation may have been, it was sufficient to keep the Japanese Islands effectively isolated culturally from such influences as did impinge. Yet one wonders how much *major* impact this nonreceptive situation could have resisted; for example, what might have happened if the adjacent Korean coast had been occupied in Jomon times by farming cultures of Chinese pattern. The cultural isolation of Japan may prove to be primarily a result of the failure of Chinese influence to penetrate Korea until a relatively late date, as noted in the preceding chapter.

A glance at a map will show that the Japanese Islands (or at least their southern portion) also lie on the margin of the Pacific world — if in fact they did not form part of it in prehistoric times. In this vast region seafaring must have reached a fairly high development thousands of years ago in order to account for the evidence of human occupation throughout the western Pacific, from the Ryukyus, Taiwan, and the Philippines on out to Micronesia. Geographically, all of these are more remote from the mainland than is Japan, yet culturally they are closer, both to the mainland and to each other. It is true that the Pacific Islanders had developed the equipment and techniques for seafaring to a high degree, whereas Jomon navigation seems to have been aimed only at offshore fisheries. Thus we need not be surprised at the lack of traces of Jomon voyagers in Taiwan or Micronesia; but the reverse should not necessarily hold. Until the archaeology of Kyushu is far better known than it is today we cannot rule out the possibility that evidence of Oceanian relationships, or at least contacts, will eventually come to light — especially in view of Professor Ono's hypothesis that a language of southern origin with a phonetic system like that of present-day Polynesian was widespread through western Japan, at least at the end of the Jomon period. This seeming isolation of southern Japan in a maritime world thus poses another major enigma. Yet recently we have been asked to see Jomon Japan as a long-range exporter of culture, albeit accidentally, without whose intervention the coastal population of distant Ecuador would have languished without the potter's art.

Turning now to the sequential development and culture history of the Jomon tradition, it has recently been suggested that the entire Jomon development can perhaps best be understood in terms of the New World theoretical concept of the area co-tradition. This appears to be perhaps the first appropriate example to be proposed from the Old World. Although the validity of this application has yet to be demonstrated, it would seem to offer at least a plausible working hypothesis. However, in view of the marked cultural differences between eastern and western Japan throughout this time span it is necessary to visualize two such co-traditions, contemporary and developing parallel to one another. To view eastern Japan as the sole Jomon nuclear area, as some have done, is to distort the picture. The existence of such Jomon area co-traditions would seem to be reflected solely in pottery complexes, but it must be realized that at present this is the only aspect of culture on which sufficient data are available. Furthermore, pottery complexes are generally considered to be the most sensitive indicators of cultural influence and change. Areally, such complexes should indicate culture areas and the extent of horizon distribution, while temporally they define the time-depth of the local tradition. Viewing the Jomon ceramic evidence from this point of view, it can be seen that from time to time certain pottery complexes spread widely, thus constituting horizon markers, and are considered to represent cultural diffusion from one or another center. In no instance do these diffusions reflect technological innovations or advances — and in fact no essential technological changes can be seen throughout the Jomon period, subsequent to the initial establishment of the tradition. It has been suggested that these evidences of cultural diffusion more likely reflect socio-economic changes or religious cult influences. For eastern Japan seven major diffusions of this nature have been proposed which alter or affect the local traditions in the various regions and create so-called "disconformities" in the latter. The spread of these diffusions affected the mixed-forest zone (the nuclear Jomon territory) and its adjacent margins, such as the Central Highlands and southwestern Hokkaido — suggesting the importance of ecological factors in the process.

The pattern of comparable processes in western Japan has not been analyzed in such detail. Given the geographical discontinuity of the area and the more varied environmental conditions, interrelationships within it were probably not always as close and direct, but broad similarities are evident even in the case of Kyushu, which not only occupies a marginal position but environmentally is probably closer to South China and southernmost Korea than to the rest of Japan. This geographical position of Kyushu as well as its environmental characteristics naturally raise the possibility of relationships with, or influences from, Korea and China on the one hand, and the Ryukyus, Taiwan, and the Pacific world on the other, as factors which might have contributed to the sometimes rather atypical nature of its ceramic complexes. These possibilities are tempting, and should certainly be kept in mind, but it must be emphasized that the available data provide no support and suggest that such factors at best played a minor role.

Northeastern Hokkaido, at the other extreme, was a world by itself from start to finish: an area of such distinctive complexes that the picture suggests long occupation by a quite different ethnic group. We shall return to the implications of this later on. It should also be noted that this northeastern half of Hokkaido might be expected, from its geographical position, to show evidence of some influences from the adjacent Siberian coast, to which the boreal environment would have been congenial. However, the earlier prehistory of the latter area is still so little known that the question cannot be explored.

After this somewhat impressionistic overview and hypothetical interpretation, a more detailed picture of Jomon culture and life is best presented in terms of the conventional five stages, bearing in mind that these have become purely arbitrary subdivisions of a continuing historical process and a basically unchanging pattern of life.

The Initial Jomon stage was the formative period for this tradition and pattern, with the basic features that were to characterize it well established by its close. Already the fundamental cultural division between eastern and western Japan — doubtless rooted in environmental and ecological factors — is evident in the basic pottery decoration techniques: typically rotary stamp (roulette) in the west (figs. 3.6, 3.7) accomplished by rolling a carved stick, and incisions made with shells in the east (fig. 3.8).

Figure 3.6. Roulette pottery from Hashidate (after Serizawa et al.).

Figure 3.7. Roulette pottery from Hashidate (after Serizawa et al.).

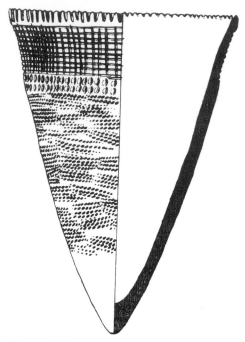

Figure 3.8. Vessel decorated with shell incisions (after Serizawa, with permission).

Most of the sites are small, suggesting temporary camps, and many are in highland areas. Though an inland-oriented life is postulated by some, the evidence of more extensive coastal exploitation may simply be lost. We don't know where the actual shore line was in the earlier phases. In general, this was the time when the sea was invading former coastal lowlands, especially in the Inland Sea region. The earliest shell middens contain shallow-water molluscs that were proliferating in these new conditions; at first they were fresh or brackish water species, gradually replaced by salt-water ones as the sea rose. The Natsushima site at the mouth of Tokyo Bay is generally viewed as reflecting the beginning of the basic Jomon economic adaptation; at least no earlier examples are yet known. And here the first settlers were living in a marsh situation. Later a real maritime situation developed, with genuine sea hunting, offshore fishing, and shore collecting. Adequate watercraft were obviously in regular use. But the Jomon ecological pattern was always a balanced one, exploiting all available resources, and there is abundant evidence of the hunting of land animals as well, chiefly deer and wild pig. Domestic dogs are also reported, and it is interesting to note that the time horizon is quite close to the early dated dogs of the Lake Baikal region in Siberia, and older than any certain evidence elsewhere.

At least one Initial Jomon site yielded the oldest stone net sinkers in Japan, indicating the introduction or invention of net fishing at this time, which we would expect to be closely associated with watercraft. Fish were also taken with spears and a variety of hooks (including composite forms) made of antler, bird bone, and the barbed spines of the sting ray. Owing to the lack of preservation of bone materials in earlier periods, we cannot be so sure that this equipment also made its first appearance at this time. Abundant arrowpoints indicate the method of hunting, and stone mortars and grinding stones at some sites evidence preparation of plant foods, probably nuts. Ground stone axes made possible the construction of boats and dwellings. We have no details of the former, but toward the middle of the stage the first remains of pit houses appear, the type of dwelling so typical of the Jomon tradition. Presumably earlier dwellings were less substantial above-ground huts, and such structures continue in use. Traces of hearths are rare, and with few exceptions seem to have been located outside the house, in contrast to later times. The pit houses at Hanawadai are shallow (twenty to thirty centimeters deep), square in form, and range in size from 3.8 to 6.5 meters on a side. There is no standard arrangement of the posts that supported the roof, but they are generally near the wall. The central portion of the floor had been

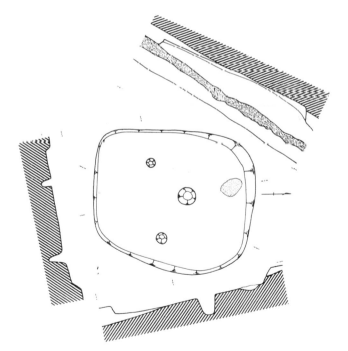

Figure 3.9. Initial Jomon dwelling: plan and cross sections (Tama New Town).

dug out more deeply than the rest. That more than one style of architecture existed even in the Kanto area is indicated by the habitations at one of the Tama New Town sites, which are also shallow but with level floors. House No. 1 here was 2.65 × 2.4 meters in size with three posts placed in a triangle supporting the roof. One post was thirty centimeters thick, the others half that size. This is one of the rare cases of a house with an interior hearth, which here was located close to the north wall. Circular pit houses are reported from Tohoku and Kyushu. It is quite possible that pit houses were already in more general use than archaeologists have thought, since their shallow depth at this stage would cause them easily to escape the notice of excavators.

The oldest clay figurines, another typical Jomon feature, make their first appearance at this time, albeit in a very crude form and small in size. Whatever intellectual concept they may reflect (they are widely assumed to have a cult character or to be in some way associated with supernaturalism) was already a part of the cultural pattern in some areas at least. Unfortunately the limited number of burials from this time add little to our understanding of ideology.

The segment of culture history labeled Early Jomon coincides with the maximum sea levels of postglacial time, resulting in transgressions in lowland coastal areas and a new positioning of their shore lines and hence of coastal habitation sites. In overall terms there was a reduction in the area of available human habitat, but what effects this may have had are unclear. If a more irregular coastline resulted, it could have been longer in actual linear dimension and hence have increased the potential for shore dwellers. Certainly there was an increase in shallow water area, which might be expected to proliferate the shellfish supply, though at the same time discouraging deep sea fishing.[2] This same general time saw the postglacial climatic optimum; in eastern and northern Japan in particular, environmental conditions for man must have been at their most favorable. It is no surprise that the stage from the beginning is marked by larger settlements and a conspicuous cultural efflorescence.

From the cultural viewpoint the stage opens with the phenomenon of widespread diffusion so that a number of traits are shared in common over a very extensive area from southern Hokkaido into the Chubu region. This is followed by a period of distinctive local cultural development in each region. The diffusion is one of ideas and techniques, which are added on to the various local traditions; nothing suggests actual movement of peoples. The conspicuous horizon marker is a technique of pottery decoration known as "feather cord rolling" (fig. 3.10), in which two knotted or looped and twisted cords were rolled horizontally over the plastic vessel surface. The source of this diffusion seems to have been the Tohoku region. Other ideas

2. It is significant in this connection that the maximum phase of the transgression coincides with a marked increase in population and a strictly littoral economy in such regions.

Figure 3.10. Decoration by "feather cord rolling" from Fujioka shell mound (after Okamoto and Tsukada).

and influences spread, though not as widely, eastwards from western Japan. Apparent now, as later, is the marked cultural frontier in the Chubu district between east and west that prevented too much sharing between the two major culture areas of Japan. Any trait that succeeded in crossing, however, was apt to spread rapidly beyond. In addition to diffusion, actual trade is suggested now. Sites in Ishikawa and Toyama prefectures on the Sea of Japan such as Sanami and Gokurakuji may have been centers of manufacture for stone earrings that were widely traded throughout much of Japan. And the distinctive Sobata type pottery of Kyushu raises the question of contacts across the strait with Korea.

Midway through the stage the first "horseshoe pattern" sites (fig. 3.11) appear, which are to be so characteristic of eastern Japan from this point on. Here the shell midden takes the form of a horseshoe, or in some cases two horseshoes placed end to end. Dwellings were arranged around the inner margins, and refuse was thrown behind them, gradually building up the midden. The central area inside the ring is free of remains, but whether it was actually kept clear at all times, or served as a sort of village plaza, as some maintain, is problematical. Attempts to estimate population or settlement size based on number of house pits or cubic content of midden (i.e., food refuse) material are unconvincing, inasmuch as sites of any size were obviously occupied over a considerable period of time and the number of dwellings in simultaneous use at any point cannot be established. To think in terms of "villages" is thus misleading.[3] In the case of a locality continuously or regularly occupied due to its strategic position with regard to food resources,

3. It has been pointed out that "horsehoe" middens are formed along the sloping edges of coastal promontories, and thus reflect preferred site location rather than any community planning or organization.

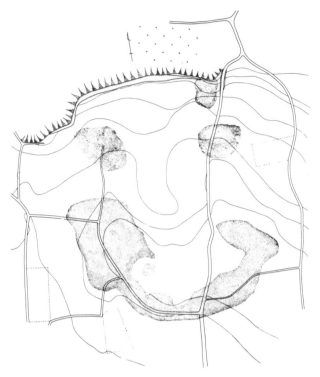

Figure 3.11. Plan of Soya shell mound: a typical "horseshoe" midden (courtesy of S. Sugihara).

even a relatively small group could produce an impressive accumulation of shells in the course of a few centuries. The majority of Early Jomon sites, though, are small "spot" middens, suggesting campsites of a small band.

Some of the pit houses discovered from this time in the Kanto region are rectangular in shape and dug deeper than previously. Those at the Fujioka site, for example, are approximately three by five meters in size, with floors about fifty centimeters below ground level. The posts supporting the super-structure had been placed around the edges of the floor, leaving the interior uncluttered. There is a basin-shaped hearth somewhat off center. However, even in the Kanto there was considerable variability, and elsewhere architecture differed as we might expect from the strong regionalism evident. Pit houses in the southern Chubu region are round and lack hearths. Those in Tokai are elliptical or squarish with rounded corners.

The oldest surviving examples of boats are from the Early Jomon period. From the Kamo site, representing a late phase, for example, come the remains of a dugout canoe and six paddles (fig. 3.12). It is believed to have originally been five to six meters long and a meter wide, with square ends. Though the

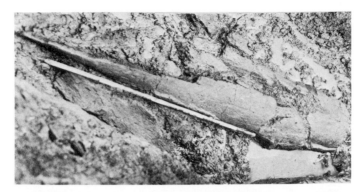

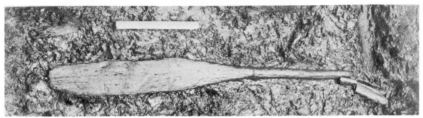

Figure 3.12. Remains of canoe (above) and paddle (below) from Kamo (after Matsumoto et al.).

surviving portion is rather shallow, there are indications that side boards may have been sewn on to the dugout hull to increase the freeboard and thus render the craft more seaworthy. Boats of this same general type are known from the coasts of Northeast Asia in historic times. The Kamo site also yielded the remains of a small, rather crude bow.

Figurines from the later Early Jomon in Tohoku are rather crude flat clay plaques with triangular bodies, to which nodes were applied to represent breasts and genitals. Invariably the heads are broken off and missing (fig. 3.13).

There is much evidence of domestic dogs, and it is of particular interest that they were buried in a number of cases in accordance with a definite ritual. Such attitudes again are reminiscent of those at Ust'-Belaia in the Baikal region of Siberia.

Middle Jomon is often viewed as a time of major cultural florescence.[4] The majority of the known Jomon sites belong to this stage, with the heaviest concentration to the east of the Kinki region. In the Kanto region at least there is a dramatic increase in the number of interior sites. Perhaps life here was

4. It is of interest that a significant change in the physical type of the population at this time is claimed by T. Ogata. The cultural inventory, however, falls within the range of variation of the existing Jomon tradition; nothing really new and different has been proven to appear during this stage.

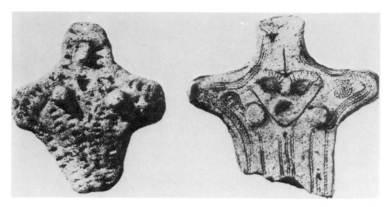

Figure 3.13. Early Jomon figurines from Tohoku (after Esaka).

now more inland-oriented, as indicated not only by the distribution of sites but also by the increase in animal bones and arrowheads found in them. Most are located on hills. However, there are also plenty of coastal sites. Shell middens from this time are found on peninsulas or on their slopes; in the latter case the people were living on top and throwing their refuse down the sides. Most sites are larger than previously, some shell middens being up to two hundred meters in diameter.

Middle Jomon might be characterized as a time of regional cultural developments on a larger scale than in the preceding stage — that is, less localized. Five such "culture areas" can be seen in the eastern region, with evidence of only limited contact and interchange between them. Since they do not seem explainable on the grounds of ecological differences, how we are to interpret them remains an open question. Some feel they represent different ethnic groups or even "tribes." General cultural efflorescence is reflected in the pottery, which has become a major art medium. Ceramics are striking in appearance, such as the Katsusaka ware, with large and richly adorned vessels typical (figs. 3.14, 3.15). J. Edward Kidder sees a change now from the purely domestic wares of the past to wares for ritual and display purposes, stressing the nonfunctional approach of Middle Jomon potters. However, it has also been pointed out that the larger vessels could have been used for storage purposes. Tsuboi even goes so far as to suggest the production now of different vessel forms for specific purposes. In addition to pottery, figurines become conspicuous, and mortuary practices are a matter of concern.

Of interest are the claims by some scholars of indications of plant cultivation in the central highland region. They point to the large, stable settlements (not convincingly proven), the processing equipment for vegetable foods such as metates, the large vessels available for storage, and the figurines which elsewhere in the world are widely associated with fertility. Further fuel for the

Figure 3.14. Katsusaka ware from Tama New Town (above) and Ubayama (below).

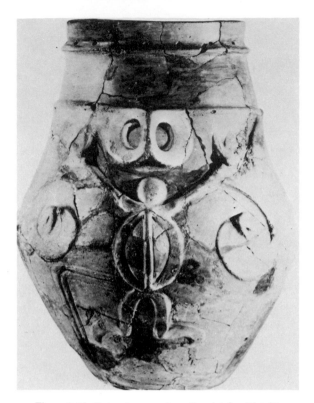

Figure 3.15. Katsusaka ware from Tonai (after Mutoh).

argument was provided by discovery of the remains of cakes of some starchy food (immediately labeled "bread") in the Sori and Tonai sites at Idojiri. However, it is curious that any such "evidence of farming" seems lacking in the following Late and Final Jomon periods of the same area, when we might more readily accept it. The "farming" sites are located in a region rich in wild plant foods, and there is good evidence of the wide use of nuts. The case of aboriginal California demonstrates that an economy in which nuts are a major staple is quite sufficient to induce and support large stable settlements, which could still carry on considerable supplementary hunting and fishing. The same type of processing equipment would also be employed. In fact, many of the arguments for Middle Jomon farming could with equal validity be employed to "prove" a farming economy in aboriginal California.[5]

5. The case is further weakened by the recent discovery of apparently similar "bread" in an Early Jomon site (Mineichigo) located in another prefecture. An analysis of a Middle Jomon example showed half of it to be composed of clay, which might or might not have been considered edible.

In general, then, the Middle Jomon economy would seem to have been one basically similar to that of the California Indians, with ample plant foods and land game, and with coastal dwellers continuing to fish and to make important use of shellfish (as was also the case in California). Domestic dogs were also on occasion eaten, as at Ubayama, a practice very widespread in East Asia in historic times.

Easternmost Japan seems to have been the only area of major fishing activity, judging by the harpoons, fish spears, and evidence of net fishing, as well as the numerous fish hooks of more elaborate type than hitherto (fig. 3.16). (Again, the northern coastal regions of California had a primarily fishing economy.)

In the southern Chubu region a typical Middle Jomon settlement would consist of twenty or so circular pit houses located on gently sloping ground overlooking a stream or perennial spring. The houses are three to four meters in diameter with floors fifty centimeters below ground level. Four or six large central posts supported the roof, and there is a rock-lined central hearth. At the famous Ubayama shell midden in coastal Kanto one type of dwelling is basically similar, but another also occurs which is square or rectangular with rounded corners and with the roof posts placed in the corners and along the margins of the pit (fig. 3.18).

The spirit of Middle Jomon life is also suggested by the abundance of ornaments in use, often made of attractive varieties of stone, including jade, otherwise of bone, antler, and shell. These include pendants, bracelets, and earrings.

The most conspicuous feature of the Late Jomon stage is the development and flourishing of the most efficient maritime cultures of the entire Jomon era, though this development is concentrated on the Pacific coast of northeastern Honshu. Curiously, it faded out in the Kanto region toward the end of the stage, raising interesting questions. The division of Japan into two major culture areas — east and west — continues to be conspicuous. In the east, sites are larger and more numerous and yield a greater abundance of artifacts, including large numbers of figurines. In the west, sites are fewer and smaller, yield less in the way of remains, and figurines are scarce. The discussion that follows will refer to eastern Japan.

Here the most typical sites of the Late stage are huge shell middens, larger and richer in finds than any previous ones. We are told that at the Ebaradai site in Chiba prefecture two cartloads of potsherds were removed from a single level in an area four by five meters in extent. Evidently the population now, at least on the coast, was living in large villages occupied for a considerable length of time. Settlements in general tend to be located on lower ground than earlier, when hilltops, peninsulas, or slopes were favored. Horseshoe-shaped middens enclosing the village are especially common around Tokyo Bay. The

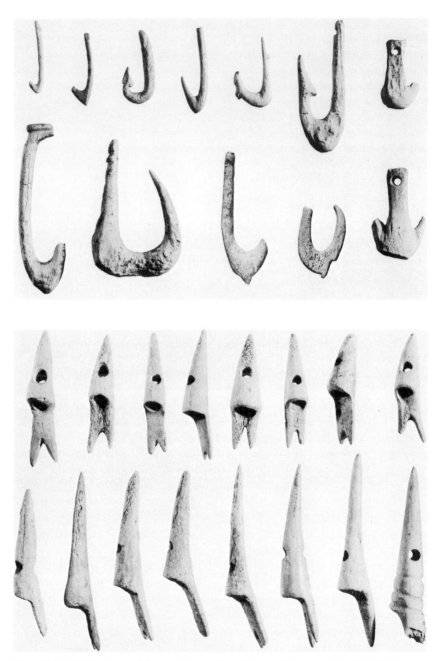

Figure 3.16. Middle Jomon fishing equipment from Numazu shell mound (Institute for Japanese Culture, Tohoku University).

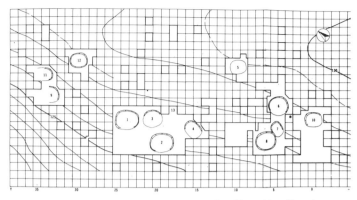

Figure 3.17. Middle Jomon settlement plan (Tama New Town).

famous Horinouchi midden here is 110–200 meters in diameter. Most dwellings seem to have been built on the surface of the ground during this stage, so that much less is known about the architecture of the time. (It is interesting that pit dwellings came back into fashion after the close of the Jomon era, in Yayoi farming settlements, and even in the protohistoric Kofun period. Obviously it is incorrect to think of them as a "primitive" type of dwelling.) Structures with flagstone floors are described from the earlier phases of the stage; sometimes these contain features which the excavators think may have

Figure 3.18. Middle Jomon house from Ubayama (courtesy of S. Sugihara).

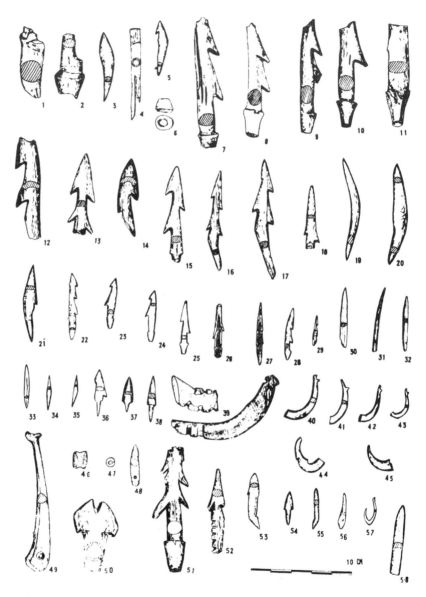

Figure 3.19. Late Jomon fishing equipment from Shomyoji shell mound (after Yoshida).

been altars. Constructions which certainly served some ceremonial function, the large circles of stones at Oyu and elsewhere in northern Honshu, are generally assigned to Late Jomon.

The greater emphasis on ocean fishing at this time may be inferred from the large coastal populations and the abundance of fishing equipment, far exceeding anything earlier. But actual maritime hunting in the sense of sea mammals also entered into the picture, and toward the end of the stage the "index fossil" of the sea hunter, the toggle harpoon, is in use on the north Pacific coast. This ingenious device has only been invented in a few areas of the world; so far, no historical connection between the occurrences has been demonstrated. In fact, the development of true maritime economic patterns is a phenomenon that has occurred only rarely in human history. The causative factors underlying these occurrences are unclear and merit further study. The Late Jomon development is one of the earliest known, and is of particular interest in that it failed to spread beyond a relatively restricted area into such suitable habitats as the Okhotsk Sea region to the north, which in later times was a major center of maritime economy. Thus, the north coast of Hokkaido had to acquire the pattern from the distant Arctic at a much later date rather than from adjacent southern Hokkaido.

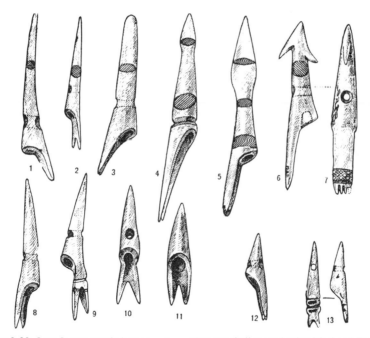

Figure 3.20. Late Jomon toggle harpoons from Numazu shell mound (after Mori and Endo).

From this general time, as indicated by its radiocarbon date of 1390 calendar years B.C., comes the Kemigawa canoe, whose paddles are considered reminiscent of South Pacific types.

Figure 3.21. Paddle from Kemigawa (after Matsumoto et al.).

The general level of cultural development is reflected in technology. Stone tools are more refined than before and appear in greater quantity (fig. 3.22). Asphalt is in use as an adhesive for hafting them and also for waterproofing purposes; it was widely traded from its sources in northern Honshu. Bone and antler artifacts are also more numerous and better made. There is a great development of ornaments toward the close of the stage: hairpins, combs, earrings, pendants, shell bracelets. Potters were producing fewer large vessels,[6] but a rich variety of forms, including spouted "teapots," plates, bottles, pedestal bowls, and effigies. Lids for vessels are typical. The "classic" Late Jomon ware is the Horinouchi (fig. 3.23), but this is always accompanied by large quantities of crude undecorated utilitarian pottery. The latter must have served the needs of daily life, lending support to the view that the fancy wares must have been manufactured for particular nonutilitarian purposes, whether these were esthetic, ritual, or a combination of both.

A great many female figurines were also made and used — for what purpose? Some types are very grotesque. In some areas, heart-shaped heads are very typical (fig. 3.24). Toward the end, pointed heads were popular in the Kanto region.

Further evidence of ritual life (or at least social custom) was the practice all over Japan at this time of knocking out certain teeth (ablation), evidently performed at puberty according to those who have studied the human remains.

Jar burial became popular, although simple interment in the midden actually continued to be the commonest treatment of the dead.

In the Final Jomon stage, the distinctive east-west division is thought possibly to have been based on differing food resources, or at least some sort of environmental or ecological factors. In the eastern nuclear area a few very large culture spheres are visible, rather than a multitude of local developments. Tohoku seems to have been the major center of radiating influences affecting eastern Japan. Cultural advances during this stage were made in pottery and art.

The Jomon potter's art reached its climax in the Kamegaoka ware, the

6. Whatever the large Middle Jomon jars had been used for, the purpose served evidently no longer existed.

Figure 3.22. Late Jomon stone tool kit from Horinouchi and Soya shell mounds (courtesy of S. Sugihara).

most refined of all, which spread widely in eastern Japan. It occurs in a rich variety of forms, and the decoration applied to the fancier pieces qualifies them to rank as real works of art by any standard. Lacquer became an important decorative medium. Figurines continue to be conspicuous (fig. 3.26). Some animal figures were also made in northern Honshu. There is a great efflorescence of polished stone tools.

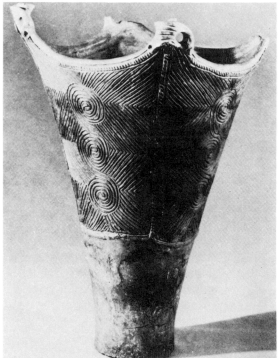

Figure 3.23. Examples of Horinouchi ware (courtesy of S. Sugihara).

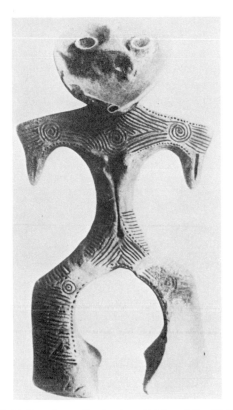

Figure 3.24. Late Jomon figurine from Satohara (after Yamayaki).

The cultural and ecological dichotomy between western and eastern Japan in Final Jomon corresponds to the subsequent areas on the one hand of rapid spread of Yayoi rice cultivation, and on the other of seeming resistance to it. Many scholars suspect that some form of cultivation may already have been present in the west, so that the region was "pre-adapted" to a farming economy. The chipped axes so prevalent here are thought by some to be digging tools. In Kyushu, rice has been found in some Final Jomon sites, but we do not know how important it was in the economy, how it was grown (wet or dry?), or where it was grown. We are completely ignorant of the history of the staple Japanese crops other than rice. All of these are *assumed* to have been introduced along with rice, but they do not necessarily fit in with the very specialized wet-rice complex.

New light has been thrown on the problem by the 1970–71 excavations in the Uenoharu site at Kumamoto, Kyushu, which is assigned on the basis of pottery types to the early phase of the Final Jomon period. Here were found remains of barley and rice of some sort. Other evidence suggests the presence of upland farming (probably of the slash-and-burn variety) before the wet-rice complex appeared in the area. Evidently the first farming in southwestern Japan was a gradual introduction of various crops which were grafted on to the existing Jomon pattern of life. What typifies the succeeding Yayoi period, in contrast, was the presence of an effective village farming pattern supplying a major part of the diet, centering on wet-land rice, and employing the techniques and equipment that have been used in Japan ever since.

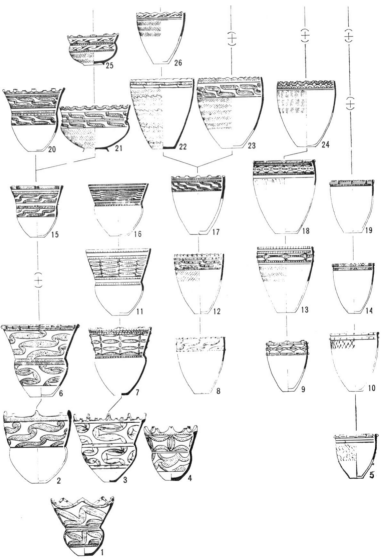

Figure 3.25. Examples of Kamegaoka ware (after Abiko).

Figure 3.26. Final Jomon figurine from Ebisuda (*Tohoku Kokogaku*, no. 1).

In the north, maritime hunting with elaborate toggle harpoons was important. Salt-making was a new development here. In the Kanto region, however, there was a steady shift away from coastal exploitation; during the later phases shell middens are virtually absent, indicating that molluscs had lost their former role in the diet. Evidently some major change in economic patterns was underway. The cultures toward the end of the stage also begin to diverge markedly from the previous tradition. Doubtless this is largely due to new cultural influences spreading eastwards from the advancing Yayoi culture, which was already established by then in southern Japan.

Viewing Jomon Japan as a whole, it is characterized by the unusually long persistence of a pattern of life and a basic cultural tradition. There is little essential technological change over the long span of time following the Initial Jomon stage when the pattern and tradition took shape. The only real innovation in later times was the invention of the toggle harpoon. There was no significant economic change, either — simply shifts in emphasis in certain regions from time to time, the only possible exception being the high development of maritime exploitation towards the end of the period; but this, again, was confined to the northeast coast. The whole picture indicates a high degree of adaptation and resistance to change. It also suggests that the attention of the Jomon people may very well have been focused on the intellectual and artistic aspects of their culture. They might, for instance, have had a highly developed social and ceremonial life like that of the Northwest Coast Indians of the New World. The stability and evident richness of Jomon life suggests this possibility.

Their essentially sedentary existence is indicated by the sheer abundance of pottery in the sites, and the presence of vessels of large size and elaborate form, not to mention the pit dwellings, heavy grinding stones, and large refuse accumulations. Seasonal interior hunting, as evidenced in bone remains, is in no way inconsistent with such a life, and can be carried out by parties from the home base. As already pointed out, the general ecological and demographic picture is strikingly reminiscent of aboriginal California, and many fruitful insights might be derived from exploring these parallels further.

One may wonder whether the littoral orientation of the total Jomon population has not been overemphasized. The shell middens (of which there are said to be 2000 in Japan — 1000 in the Kanto area alone) bulk large in the archaeological record due to ease of discovery, concentration of materials, and the high degree of preservation of remains found in them. Actually, however, they comprise only a small percentage of known Jomon sites, let alone the countless others that must have been destroyed in the course of many centuries of intensive human exploitation of the soil of Japan. These shell middens are simply the refuse heaps of settlements, though easily confused with the settlement itself. They are not necessarily coterminous with the latter, and even an impressive midden may have been associated, at any one point in time, with a rather modest community.

Regionalism, both on a large scale and in a more localized sense, is also a conspicuous characteristic of Jomon Japan. We do not really know how to interpret its significance. At the same time, there were common features widely shared. As Kamaki (1965) has said,

> The people who produced Jomon culture had both local variations and common bases beyond these local variations. We still do not know whether these common bases were reflections of a similar economic base, and thereby a similar social structure, throughout the various localities, or whether local differences were based upon different customs and manners although the social structure was the same in various areas. . . . The complexity of local variations is one of the features unique to Jomon culture in comparison with other cultures.

As for the Jomon population of Japan itself, the interpretation of the human remains has long been a source of controversy that in general has generated more heat than light. Three main viewpoints have been that they were the ancestors of the modern Ainu, the ancestors of the modern Japanese, or a population essentially distinct from both. Recent studies by William W. Howells show that Jomon remains exhibit considerable variation but could not be included within the range of variation of either the modern Ainu or the modern Japanese. By and large they are decidedly non-Japanese, suggesting little genetic continuity into historic times, except perhaps locally. They are generally less "Mongoloid," and in other ways as well are more reminiscent of Ainu. Howells suggests that the Jomon people constituted varied tribal populations, perhaps much as American Indians did. The modern Ainu are doubtless one survivor of these, but they were not the only such population nor even a typical one. There is no evidence that people of Ainu type occupied any of the Japanese Islands except Hokkaido prior to medieval times.

It has already been pointed out that northeastern Hokkaido remained culturally aberrant throughout the Jomon era and afterwards — a situation suggesting long occupation of this area by an ethnic group that felt itself to be different. Available evidence indicates that the historic Ainu as a genetic entity were indigenous to the general area and that their forebears must therefore be reflected in some of the prehistoric complexes of Hokkaido. It seems plausible to postulate precisely this distinctive region as the likely original Ainu homeland.

Hokkaido lay too far to the north to be affected by the spread of the Yayoi farming culture that transformed the economy and pattern of life of all the rest of Japan. Only in modern times has rice cultivation been successfully established. Thus we find the Jomon way of life and Jomon cultural traditions lingering on in the northern island after their disappearance elsewhere. The label "Epi-Jomon" is applied to such manifestations. The final prehistoric period in Hokkaido presents a striking dichotomy between the maritime Okhotsk culture of the northern coast and the interior culture of land hunting and river fishing which goes under the name of Satsumon. The Okhotsk sea hunters were an intrusive people from Sakhalin whose ultimate origins lay far to the north. Theirs was the first maritime culture on the northern coast of Hokkaido, for, curiously, the earlier maritime economic complexes in the southern part of the island had never spread farther north into what might seem an optimum niche. It is obvious that the immediate ancestors of the Ainu whom we know peopled the entire island soon afterwards at the dawn of history must have been present in Satsumon times, since there is no outside source from which they could have arrived subsequently. Though we do not know the bearers of the Satsumon culture, they could only have been the Ainu, since the contemporary Okhotsk population (the only alternative) is of totally different physical type.

Bibliography

Befu, Harumi, and Chard, Chester S.
    1964. "A prehistoric Maritime Culture of the Okhotsk Sea." *American
        Antiquity* 30: 1–18.
Chard, Chester S.
    1972. "Prehistoric Japan: A Survey of Cultural Development Down to the
        Late Jomon Stage." In *Early Chinese Art and Its Possible Influence in
        the Pacific Basin*, edited by N. Barnard, 2: 373–93. New York: Inter-
        cultural Arts Press.
Howells, William W.
    1966. "The Jomon Population of Japan." *Papers of the Peabody Museum
        of Archaeology and Ethnology, Harvard University* 57: 3–43.
Ikawa, Fumiko
    1964. "The Continuity of Non-Ceramic to Ceramic Cultures in Japan."
        Arctic Anthropology 2, no. 2: 95–119.
Kamaki, Yoshimasa, ed.
    1965. *Nihon no Kokogaku, 2: Jomon Jidai*. Tokyo: Kawade Shobo Shinsha.
Kidder, J. Edward
    1966. *Japan before Buddhism*. Rev. ed. New York: Praeger.
    1968. *Prehistoric Japanese Arts: Jomon Pottery*. Tokyo and Palto Alto:
        Kodansha International Ltd.
Morlan, Richard E.
    1967. "Chronometric Dating in Japan." *Arctic Anthropology* 4, no. 2:
        180–211.
Ono, Susumu
    1962. "The Japanese Language: Its Origin and Its Sources." In *Japanese
        Culture: Its Development and Characteristics*, edited by Robert J.
        Smith and Richard K. Beardsley, pp. 17–21. Chicago: Aldine.
Yamanouchi, Sugao, ed.
    1964. *Nihon Genshi Bijutsu*. Tokyo: Kodansha.
Yawata, Ichiro, ed.
    1960. *Sekai Kokogaku Taikei*. Vol. 1. Tokyo: Heibonsha.

4 The Steppes of Inner Asia

As pointed out earlier, the pattern of life in the forest zone of Siberia remained essentially unchanged from early post-glacial times down until European contact. This was not due to "backwardness" or to complete isolation from the transformations going on elsewhere — witness the introduction of metal, however limited — but was the result of environmental conditions, which ruled out farming until modern times. The forest thus perforce remained a world apart. But not so the forest-steppe and steppe zones across the southern margin of Siberia, which were able to share in the transformation of the rest of Asia.

The first food production appeared in the western half of the steppe and forest steppe, as far east as the Yenisei valley, probably toward the end of the third millennium B.C. It was introduced by a people of European racial type who were the bearers of the Afanasievo culture. There is reason to believe that they spoke an ancestral form of Indo-European. Related cultures are found on the lower Volga (earliest stage of the Kurgan culture) and on the Aral Sea (later stages of the Kel'teminar culture). It may be presumed that the food-producing pattern of the steppe developed in the latter areas and spread both east and west. Afanasievo pottery shows strong similarity to Kel'teminar, and ornaments in burials include shells which could only have been obtained from the Aral Sea. The wide dispersal of these related groups suggests considerable mobility.

The Afanasievo people were stock breeders (cattle, sheep, horses), but still engaged in a considerable amount of hunting. No direct evidence of farming has yet come to light, but it is suspected. Most sites are burial places under low mounds (kurgans) surrounded by circular stone walls and are associated with dentate stamped pottery. Technology was still based on stone and bone, although there are a few copper ornaments.

The Minusinsk basin, an island of steppe on the upper middle Yenisei surrounded by forested mountains, was on occasion the scene of special developments, while on others it formed part of the larger steppe world to which it was connected by a narrow corridor. One such development occurred at this time, when the Afanasievo population seems to have been supplanted by an alien group from the adjacent forest zone, whose culture is labeled

145

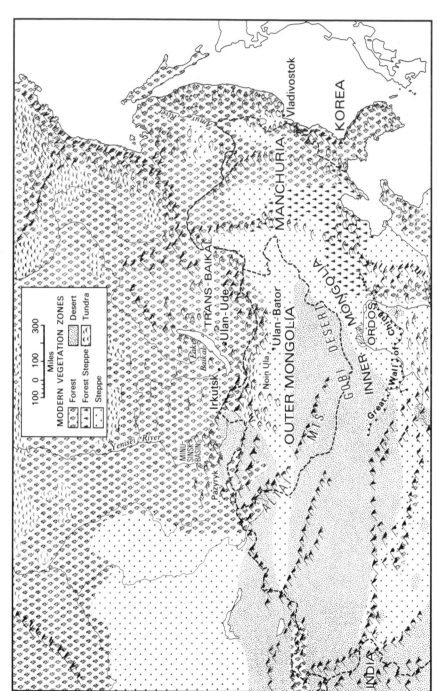

Map 5. The steppe zone of Inner Asia, showing modern vegetation zones.

MODERN VEGETATION ZONES

Forest Desert

Forest Steppe Tundra

Steppe

Miles

100 0 100 300

Yenisei River

MINU-
SINSK
BASIN

Pazyryk

Irkutsk

Lake
Baikal

Ulan-Ude

TRANS-BAIKAL

Noin Ula

Ulan-Bator

OUTER MONGOLIA

ALTAI M.T.S.

GOBI DESERT

INNER
MONGOLIA

ORDOS

Great Wall of China

INDIA

MANCHURIA

Amur River

Vladivostok

KOREA

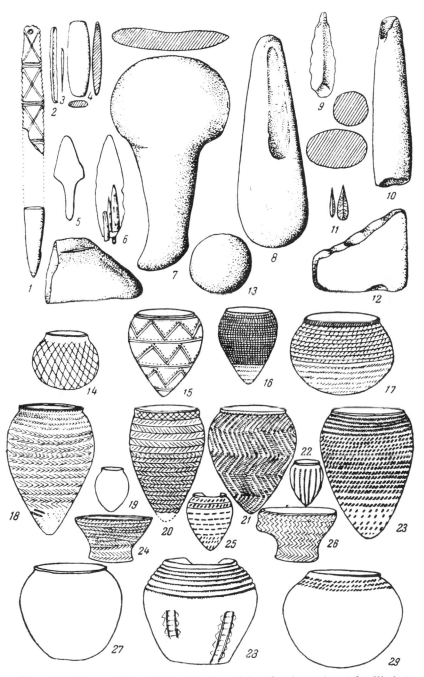

Figure 4.1. Representative artifacts and pottery of the Afanasievo culture (after Kiselev).

Okunevo. They are known from burials distributed all over the Minusinsk basin, many of which are intrusive in the Afanasievo kurgans. Knowledge of their economy and culture is thus limited, but they appear to have taken over domestic animals from the Afanasievo and to have practiced a rudimentary bronze metallurgy. Their chief significance for prehistory lies in their rich art, which was carved from or engraved on stone and bone. It is a realistic art featuring human and animal motifs (albeit the predatory creatures shown are imaginary ones) and may well be one of the major roots from which later developed the famous Scytho-Siberian animal style of the steppes — one of the great art traditions of the world.

Metallurgy became well established in the succeeding Andronovo culture (mid-second millennium B.C.). The Altai was an important source of ores and naturally became the major hearth of metal industry in Siberia. Andronovo represented the eastern half of a belt of fundamentally similar culture (and evidently related peoples) stretching across the steppe from the Don to the Yenisei, but with local features in different regions resulting mainly from contacts in each case with quite different neighbors. The western portion of the belt was occupied by the Timber Grave culture, generally considered to represent the ancestors of the Scythians. In the Andronovo culture we may see the ancestors of the related peoples who later roamed the Central Asiatic and Siberian steppes. The entire belt doubtless embodied the Indo-Iranian branch of the Indo-European language family. On the Yenisei they appear as invad-

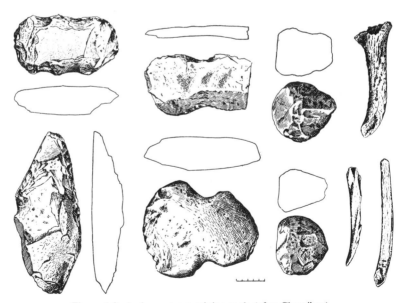

Figure 4.2. Andronovo ore mining tools (after Chernikov).

ers from the west. The Andronovo people were not nomads: they lived in stable settlements of up to ten semi-subterranean houses of log cabin construction ranging in size from sixty by thirty meters to thirty by twenty meters, grew wheat and millet, and bred sufficient livestock to supply their meat requirements. Cattle were consumed most frequently, sheep and horses next, and pigs the least. However, the ordinary diet may have consisted mostly of cereals and dairy products, to judge from the pottery vessels placed in the graves, which must have held food for the dead. Meat was not usually included and may have been eaten only on festive occasions. The most common remains are the burial places — stone enclosures with underground tombs of log-cabin construction having jointed corners and gabled roofs, or else stone cists. These burials provide the first evidence of social stratification.

In the thirteenth century B.C. the Karasuk culture developed out of the Andronovo in the same areas, with a number of local variants assumed to correspond to separate tribes. The older view that Karasuk represented an intrusive culture and population from the Ordos region, heavily Chinese-influenced, is no longer tenable. For example, the "index fossil" — the highly distinctive Karasuk bronze knife or dagger — can now be shown to have local antecedents. Neither the pottery nor the burial practices occur east of the Yenisei. Although Mongoloid elements now appear in the Yenisei population, these are not considered to be of East Asian type but are thought to stem primarily from Central Asia to the southwest; by and large there is considerable continuity from preceding times. There is evidence of contacts with China, which is scarcely surprising, but no closer relationship.

It is thought that a shift took place at this time to seasonal transhumance and a semi-nomadic pattern of life which would correspond to the primary role of sheep-raising in the economy. Evidence of early irrigation systems in the Minusinsk basin have also been ascribed to this period, and the only two known settlements contain pit houses 150–160 square meters in size. This is not necessarily contradictory, but suggests that our picture of Karasuk life is not yet clear enough for firm conclusions. The overwhelming majority of remains are burials in stone cists generally covered by a low mound but always surrounded by a usually square stone enclosure. The deceased was invariably provided with certain definite portions of a sheep (occasionally replaced by a steer or horse). The large size of the Karasuk cemeteries has been interpreted as reflecting their use of larger, long-term settlements at this time, though perhaps only seasonally occupied. If so, the remains of these settlements are not in evidence.

Despite any possible shift in the pattern of life, there is considerable continuity from the past in many aspects of culture. Metallurgy is on a much larger scale, and large quantities of distinctive bronze artifacts have been recovered, though the majority are undocumented finds. Woolen textiles are

Figure 4.3. Andronovo pottery from the Altai and Yenisei (after Komarova).

evidenced, but garments were also made of skin and furs. Remains of bridles in the later stages of the Karasuk period indicate the beginning of horse riding on the Siberian steppe.

The realistic animal art which first appeared among the earlier Okunevo people undergoes further development now and is a very conspicuous feature of the Karasuk culture. It most commonly takes the form of adornment on bronze artifacts, although we must assume that it was widely applied to perishable materials as well (as was the case later), and hence that only a minor portion of their artistic world survives.

Most of our knowledge of the steppe metal-using cultures — who are also the food-producers — came originally from the Minusinsk basin, the richest archaeological zone in Siberia and one with few equals elsewhere. The number of burial mounds covering this relatively small island of steppe is well nigh incredible. Some 40,000 bronze objects of all periods survive in collections — and this must be assumed to represent only a small percentage of the original finds from several centuries of looting. The remainder has been dispersed or melted down. Modern scientific fieldwork has on the other hand been focused primarily on the Altai region, which has suffered less depredation; but the Minusinsk materials continue to be a source of study, and extensive excavation has been resumed recently along the Yenisei, where a considerable area is to be inundated by a reservoir.

The period embracing the seventh century B.C. through the first century A.D. is known as Early Nomad, except in the Minusinsk basin, where local conditions did not promote development of the full nomad pattern. Here a

Figure 4.4. Andronovo stone burial cist (after Chernikov).

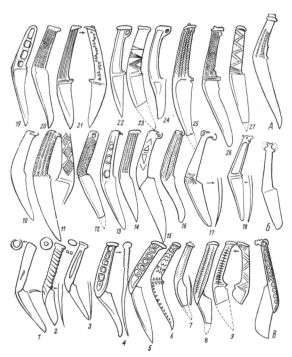

Figure 4.5. Karasuk bronze knives (after Novgorodova).

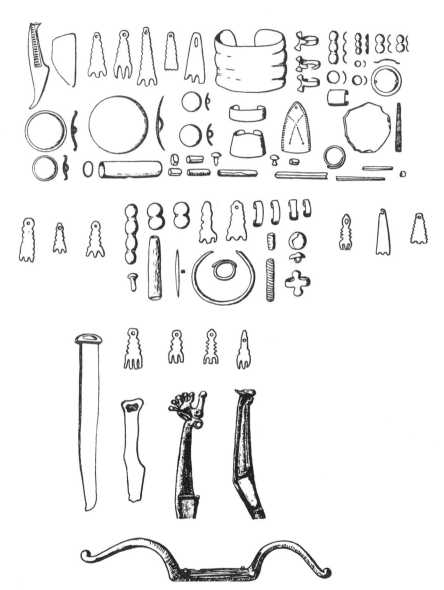

Figure 4.6. Karasuk bronze ornaments and artifacts from the Minusinsk Basin (after Kiselev).

related culture called Tagar held sway. Pastoral nomadism, one of man's major economic-ecological adaptations, which made possible effective exploitation of the grasslands for the first time, had arisen somewhere in the Central Asian steppe to the south c. 1400 B.C. or soon after and spread relatively rapidly throughout the Eurasian steppe zone, sparked apparently by the invention of horseback riding, which supplied the necessary mobility. It was established in Southern Siberia by 700 B.C. The subsequent picture of cultural development in the Altai center of metallurgy and contiguous regions such as the upper Yenisei and Minusinsk basin is complex and well known due to the abundance and richness of the archaeological remains. No other part of Siberia has been subjected to such extensive modern study. Although numerous cultural and chronological subdivisions are recognized during this Early Nomad period, the basic pattern of life remained the same and will be sketched only in general outline. There was marked cultural homogeneity at this time throughout the Eurasian steppe world, so that life in the Altai region has much in common with that of the Scythians of southern Russia. We can view these people as being at least the cultural ancestors of the historic and recent pastoralists of the steppes of central Eurasia.

Initially, the upper Yenisei valley still formed the eastern frontier of peoples of European racial type. Significant Mongoloid admixture becomes apparent in the fifth to third centuries B.C., and by the early years of the Christian era the population of the Siberian steppe is basically Mongoloid. During the fourth through the second centuries B.C. iron finally replaced bronze as the standard metal, a process that had taken place several centuries earlier among the Scythians. The time lag is probably explained by the very high quality of Altai bronze, which offered little inducement to change until iron-working had attained a comparable level locally.The economy and way of life had been transformed by the seventh century: people lived in wagons and tents, moving with the needs of the flocks and herds. Trade and contacts were very wide-ranging as a consequence of this mobility; warfare was also endemic. The mounted warrior of the steppes, a new phenomenon on the battlefields of the world, enjoyed a military superiority enabling him to exert an influence on the course of history out of all proportion to his numbers or level of cultural-technological development. The established civilizations, from China to the Near East and Europe, were faced with a continual threat and a major problem, of which the Great Wall of China remains as a striking symbol. Although the nomads of southern Siberia were remote from these historical battlefields, it is quite evident that their lives were no less filled with martial exploits.

Social stratification was highly developed, as evidenced by burial practices. The "ordinary" mounted warrior, or his wife, was interred in a log tomb under a small mound (kurgan), always with at least one fully equipped horse beside or above the tomb. Men were buried with all their weapons, women with a mirror and knife. The ornaments which decorated their clothing survive, with the jars for food and the remains of a tail-cut of mutton: evidently the fat-tailed sheep was already the preferred meat of the steppe, as it is today, and the tail the choicest portion.

The chief or other exalted personage enjoyed a much larger (though basically similar) tomb and much richer furnishings. The grave pit is four to seven meters deep and six to seven meters square, the southern half being occupied by a substantial log structure and the northern half containing from five to twenty-two richly equipped horses of prized Central Asian breeds — very different from the rugged local ponies of the modest graves (figs. 4.9–4.11). After the grave pit had been filled in, it was covered with a mound of large stones. Some 3000 man-days of labor would have been involved altogether, attesting the resources and socio-political power available. Considering the time factor, it is not surprising that mummification was practiced in such cases. These princely tombs always contain the remains of a man and woman in a massive log sarcophagus (fig. 4.13); presumably the woman had been put to death to accompany her husband, an old Indo-European practice. Although all known examples of such tombs were very promptly looted of valuables

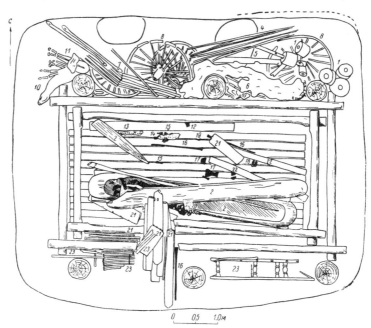

Figure 4.7. Fifth Pazyryk kurgan: plan of grave pit viewed from above, showing log coffin and separate area for horses and wagon (after Rudenko).

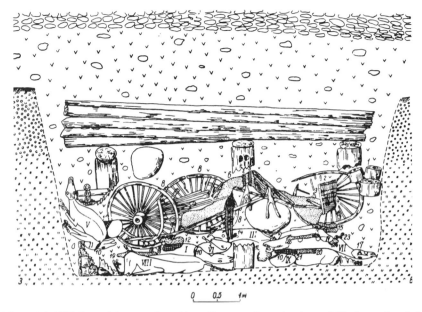

Figure 4.8. Fifth Pazyryk kurgan; disposition of horses and associated material in the north end of the grave pit (after Rudenko).

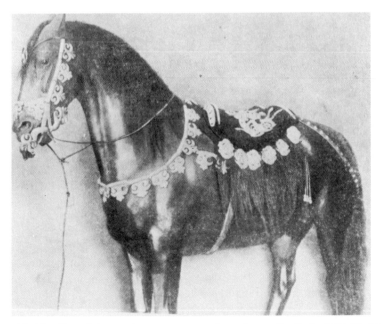

Figure 4.9. First Pazyryk kurgan: horse gear mounted on a dummy for display (after Rudenko).

Figure 4.10. First Pazyryk kurgan: mask-headdresses for horses. Left, reindeer; right, griffin (after Rudenko).

soon after interment, much remains for the archaeologist, especially in those cases where peculiar local conditions had caused the formation of permanent ice (fig. 4.14). Here perishables such as felt carpets, clothing, and leather-work survived (fig. 4.15), not to mention the tattooing on a chieftain and the stomach contents of his horses.[1] Virtually all objects of local manufacture are richly decorated in the Scytho-Siberian animal style (figs. 4.17–4.21). In addition there are many evidently treasured items imported from China, Central Asia, and Iran, including the oldest pile carpet in existence.

During this same time in the somewhat isolated Minusinsk basin where space did not permit the development of the typical nomad pattern there flourished the distinctive Tagar culture, which had strong local roots but shared in many features of the steppe world such as the animal style art. The

1. The reader is urged to consult Karl Jettmar's *Art of the Steppes*, pp. 89–111, for a detailed and dramatic account of the contents of the Second Kurgan at Pazyryk.

Figure 4.11. Fifth Pazyryk kurgan: reconstructed wagon (after Rudenko).

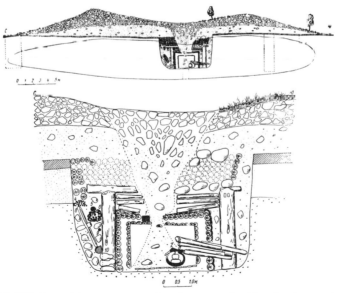

Figure 4.12. Fifth Pazyryk kurgan: cross section of stone tumulus (above) and grave pit (below), showing hole made by robbers (after Rudenko).

Figure 4.13. Second Bashadar kurgan: log coffin (after Rudenko).

Figure 4.14. Fifth Pazyryk kurgan: mummified male burial (after Rudenko).

Figure 4.15. Fifth Pazyryk kurgan: restoration of felt carpet (after Rudenko).

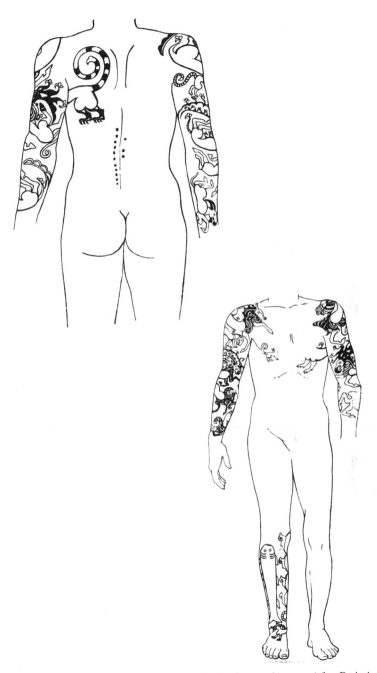

Figure 4.16. Second Pazyryk kurgan: tatooing in animal style on male corpse (after Rudenko).

Figure 4.17. First Pazyryk kurgan: saddle (side view) (after Rudenko).

Figure 4.18. First Pazyryk kurgan: decoration from a saddle covering (after Rudenko).

Figure 4.19. Second Pazyryk kurgan: decoration from a saddle covering (after Rudenko).

Figure 4.20. Fourth Pazyryk kurgan: wooden bridle pendant in form of a cat (after Rudenko).

earlier stages are represented by tens of thousands of kurgans which used large stone slabs in their construction (fig. 4.22). In the later stage the practice of collective burial for the common people arose or was introduced, coinciding with the replacement of bronze by iron. The underground tombs are, in fact, ossuaries for the bones of large numbers of individuals who were evidently first exposed, then interred secondarily over a long period of time. Some of

Figure 4.21. Gold ornament in classical animal style: griffin attacking horse. Siberian Collection of Peter I (after Rudenko).

Figure 4.22. Tagar kurgans from Minusinsk Basin (after Kiselev).

the skulls have plaster portrait masks. When the underground log chambers were eventually filled, they were set on fire and sealed up.

In the early centuries of the Christian era the Minusinsk basin gravitated towards the world to the east. There may have been an invasion from the eastern steppes at this time, although the practice of cremation makes this difficult to determine. Some Chinese influence is evident, although this doubt-less came via the Hsiung-nu in Mongolia. The cultural period at this time, known as Tashtyk, placed great stress on funerary art, including death masks and animal statues (fig. 4.24). The general pattern of life remained as before. The sixth century A.D. saw the formation of the Turk khanate centering on the Altai, which was henceforth regarded as their homeland. They are thought to have moved west from Mongolia, where their runic script occurs on monu-ments. A group closely related culturally, the Kurykan, settled in the Lake

Baikal area probably at this same general time, in patches of open country amid the forest, where they built fortified settlements, farmed, and raised cattle. They were evidently the ancestors of the Yakut, later to move still farther north and settle in the Lena valley, where they clung to the stock-raising life of the distant steppe, despite its incongruity in this arctic environment, down to the present day.

In Trans-Baikal and northern Mongolia the first food-producers of whom we have evidence are stock-raising, horse-riding nomads, dating from some time in the first millennium B.C. There is no trace of a farming stage here, as

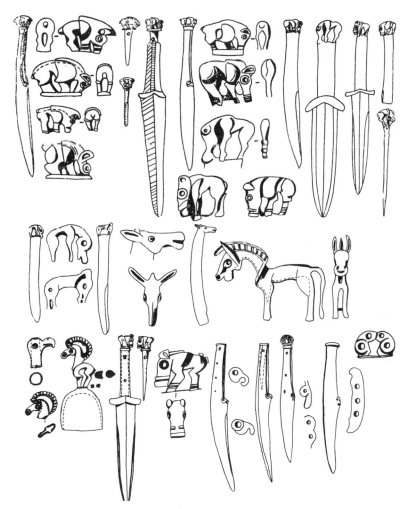

Figure 4.23. Tagar bronze artifacts in the animal style (after Chlenova).

Figure 4.24. Tashtyk funerary mask (after Kiselev).

on the western steppe. Since the population involved is of local Mongoloid type, it may be hypothesized that the pastoral pattern was borrowed from the west and adopted by a hunting population at this relatively late date. This is a rare case of a direct transition from hunting to pastoralism: a process often propounded in earlier evolutionary theory but widely contradicted by archaeology. It also indicates that the eastward spread of the steppe food-production pattern was halted at the Yenisei for perhaps 1500 years, although other cultural elements percolated through, posing interesting problems for the student of culture process.

Although the nomads of the eastern steppes show much evidence of trade and contact with their western counterparts, from whom their livestock and way of life must have come, they are culturally distinct. In particular, they differ markedly in burial practices — and most archaeological remains here are burials also. On the eastern steppes there are no kurgans at this time: the typical burials are in so-called slab graves: rectangular enclosures of stone slabs set on edge, sometimes grouped in cemeteries (fig. 4.25). There is no difference in the size of individual graves; any larger ones are collective burials. Evidently the social system characteristic of the west did not prevail here. The Trans-Baikal region is rich in ores and understandably became the focus of a well-developed local metallurgy with its own features. Chinese contact is indicated by tripod pottery vessels of *li* type — the first sign of Chinese influence north of the Gobi.

In the second century B.C. this area was taken over by the Hsiung-nu, the first major political power to develop on the eastern steppe and seriously threaten the Chinese empire. Iron became predominant at this time. Trans-Baikal was evidently the northern frontier of the Hsiung-nu state against hostile neighbors, as evidenced by the strongly fortified site of Ivolga near Ulan-Ude. This is the first Hsiung-nu settlement ever to be studied, and provides the first factual evidence of their life and culture. The fortifications consist of four lines of walls and ditches enclosing an area of over 72,000 square meters which contains many structures. Chinese engineering and workmanship is clearly evident, and the millet farming carried on here was very likely done by Chinese slaves.

Farther south in Mongolia itself are the famous "royal" tombs of Noin Ula, dated to the first century A.D., evidently the burials of high-ranking notables if not of the Hsiung-nu rulers themselves. The tombs are quite different from those of the Altai: they are found up to ten meters below ground, reached originally by a sloping ramp, and covered with a low earth mound. Much of the contents is of Chinese origin or at least Chinese work-

Figure 4.25. Slab grave on Mongolian steppe (photograph by C. S. Chard).

manship, and local products are of inferior quality. Obviously, the elite looked to China as their model. Horses are represented only by skulls, and women were permitted to donate their pigtails rather than their lives. As with the Altai tombs, those at Noin Ula had been looted at an early date, but ground water and permafrost permitted preservation of many remaining perishables. The same general pattern of Chinese influence and social stratification is reflected in more modest graves attributed to the Hsiung-nu.

Inner Mongolia, forming the northern frontier of the Chinese Neolithic farmers, came under their influence at an early date. The evidence indicates that farming, along with Yangshao technology and pottery, was introduced among or borrowed by the hunting-gathering population of this region. Later, perhaps with the onset of more arid climatic conditions, it seems to have been replaced by the steppe nomad pattern — possibly at the time this appeared in northern Mongolia from the west.

In southern and southwestern Manchuria, farming also seems to have been introduced in Yangshao times, and millet farming had at least spread to the middle Amur before the end of the Neolithic, as it seems to have to Korea also. But for the Soviet Far East in general a real transformation to food production appears to be associated with the spread of iron technology. In the Vladivostok area, domestic animals were an important part of the economy in the tenth century B.C., although agriculture is problematical. Iron was in use then (Sidemi culture). Subsequent populations were certainly farming, as were all iron-using groups on the Amur.

Bibliography

Gryaznov, Mikhail
        1969. *Southern Siberia*. Geneva: Nagel.
Istoriia Sibiri [History of Siberia].
        1968. Vol. 1. Leningrad: Nauka.
Jettmar, Karl
        1967. *Art of the Steppes*. New York: Crown Publishers.
Okladnikov, A. P.
        1964. "Ancient Population of Siberia and Its Culture." In *The Peoples of Siberia*, edited by M. G. Levin and L. P. Potapov, pp. 13–98. Chicago: University of Chicago Press.
Rudenko, S. I.
        1962. *Kul'tura Khunnov i Noinulinskie kurgany* [The Culture of the Huns and the Noin Ula Tombs]. Moscow and Leningrad: Akademiia Nauk SSSR.
        1970. *Frozen Tombs of Siberia*. Berkeley and Los Angeles: University of California Press.

5 Japan: Yayoi and Kofun

The transformation of Japan to a new way of life took place during the chronological and cultural period known as Yayoi — a brief but well-defined era of Japanese prehistory. It began about 400 B.C. with what is generally thought to be the sudden appearance of a specific cultural complex which was new to Japan. After first appearing in Kyushu, this complex spread eastward. Within the next two hundred or so years it had reached the Kinki district and had completely altered the indigenous cultures of western Japan while itself undergoing various developments and elaborations. After passing central Honshu the spread was less vigorous and the basic Yayoi complex was slightly altered. Its influence was, however, irresistible. By about 300 A.D., when Yayoi culture had completed its spread and had altered all local cultures south of Hokkaido to a basically Yayoi pattern, social and political developments in western Japan gave rise to new classes of archaeological remains which mark the end of the Yayoi period. The social elaborations which were responsible for these new features lie at the base of historic Japanese civilization.

The origin of the Yayoi cultural complex is a problem in East Asian prehistory that will not be answered ultimately until all of the areas which could have contributed to its formation are more fully known. Although all authorities agree that the Yayoi period was initiated in northern Kyushu about 400 B.C. with what we will call the Itazuke phase, there is no such agreement as to the key and defining elements of the Yayoi cultural complex. According to a leading authority, S. Sugihara, at about this time several sites in northern Kyushu which are associated with the Itazuke ceramic assemblage show evidence of the presence of farming, iron tools, and weaving. He adds that these are traits common to all Yayoi cultures, and ones which cannot be drawn from preceding Jomon cultures. On this basis he assigns the sites to the opening of the Yayoi period. Sugihara's definition is very precise and focuses on elements which apparently appeared together in Japan for the first time during the Itazuke phase. His criteria thus clearly serve to separate Yayoi and Jomon cultures. The time period we are calling the Itazuke phase is represented by several sites in northern Kyushu which are associated with the Itazuke ceramic complex. The type site for this ceramic complex, the Itazuke site, is located in

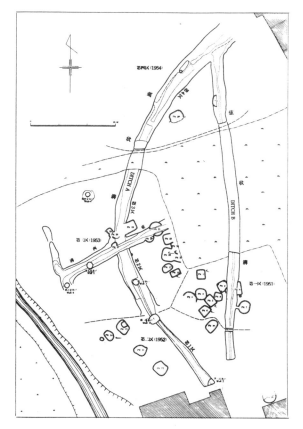

Figure 5.1. Plan of Itazuke site (Sugihara, 1961, by permission).

northeastern Fukuoka prefecture Sugihara considers the Itazuke site to be the oldest farming community known from Japan. It is located on a small terrace at the side of a low hill which is surrounded by a flat alluvial plain now covered with wet rice paddies. Apparently at the time the site was occupied much of this plain was low and swampy. This situation is characteristic of many Early Yayoi sites.

There can be no doubt that the occupants of Itazuke drew a part of their subsistence from cultivated rice (*Oriza sativa*). Carbonized grains of rice have been found at this and other Itazuke phase sites. Furthermore, impressions of rice grains are regularly noted as appearing in the bases and walls of Itazuke pots. The fact that no paddy fields or irrigation works can be assigned to the Itazuke phase or to any Early Yayoi site suggests that at this time rice seeds may have been sown in naturally swampy areas; as a result, their germination could not be controlled and yields were low.

The ceramic assemblages from the Itazuke site and its contemporaries can be described as having two facies. One of these, which is clearly a product of the local Jomon ceramic tradition, can be called Yusu ware after a site in Fukuoka prefecture (fig. 5.2). The other facies of the assemblage can itself be called the Itazuke ware, and most Japanese archaeologists believe that it includes attributes which were new to Japan and which therefore attest outside cultural influence (fig. 5.3). The important point to be made here is that these two invariably appear together in sites throughout Kyushu. The two together form the total Itazuke ceramic complex which serves to define the Itazuke phase.

As with pottery, the stone artifacts from the Itazuke site can be divided into Jomon and "non-Jomon" groups. The typically Jomon artifacts account for about half of the nonceramic artifacts from the site. Artifacts which are not typical of preceding Jomon assemblages include several fired-clay spindle whorls and a large polished stone inventory of heavy biconvex celts, beveled and asymetrical adzes, daggers, tanged points, and double-perforated, semilunar rice sickles, or *ishibocho*. The total tool assemblage from the type site thus indicates that hunting, spinning, wood working, and farming were all important during the Itazuke phase.

The society of the Itazuke phase appears to have been fairly simple. In

Figure 5.2. Yusu ware from the Itazuke site (Sugihara, 1961, by permission).

Figure 5.3. Itazuke ware from the Itazuke site (Sugihara, 1961, by permission).

spite of the advent of rice agriculture there was no apparent increase in population over the Jomon period levels: the number of sites and their distribution seems basically unchanged from the Final Jomon period. The habitation sites from the phase possess none of the signs of ordered village life that are to be seen in some subsequent large Yayoi sites. Certainly the features seen at Itazuke suggest some communal effort, but such things as large-scale irrigation projects do not appear until later. Likewise, there is no sign of the areal interdependence which seems a characteristic of the later Yayoi period. If there was social stratification during the Itazuke phase it was poorly developed and only weakly reflected in burial practices. The range of sites created during the phase presents a picture of a mixed economy based on primitive rice agriculture and hunting and gathering. It is quite possible that the primitive farming techniques used at the time gave such a low yield that the economy was forced to fall back on traditional gathering techniques. An alternative explanation might be that a basically hunting and gathering culture had not at this time fully adopted an agricultural life. There is no evidence to rule out the possibility that during the Itazuke phase primitive rice agriculture was just one seasonal activity of groups that at other times exploited wild food resources.

Of the diagnostic Yayoi traits, iron tools and spindle whorls seem

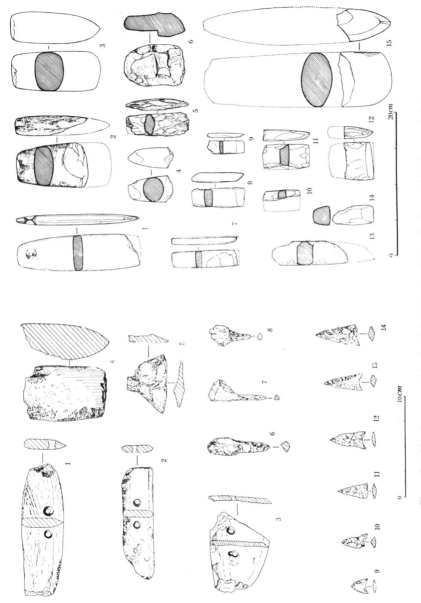

Figure 5.4. Yayoi stone tool kit. Top left, *ishiboc*h*o* sickles (Sugihara, 1961, by permission).

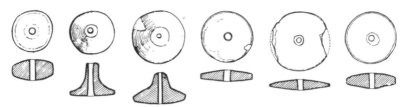

Figure 5.5. Early Yayoi spindle whorls (Sugihara, 1961, by permission).

definitely to have appeared in Japan for the first time during the Itazuke phase. However, the great majority of the characteristics of the Itazuke-phase ceramics can be derived from the preceding Jomon tradition.

Perhaps the clearest evidence of outside influence on Japan during the Itazuke phase is seen in the stone tool assemblage. Although polished stone adzes and other polished stone tools are found in Final Jomon sites of Kyushu, the perforated semi-lunar *ishibocho*, tanged polished points, daggers, and several other forms appear for the first time in Japan now. The few iron tools known from the phase must reflect actual trade with the continent.

In summary, the Itazuke phase can be considered as the first manifestation of the Yayoi period, since in addition to many indigenous (Jomon) traits it shows prominent rice agriculture, weaving, and iron tools — elements which must have been introduced from outside of Japan and which Sugihara and other authorities consider to lie at the base of subsequent Yayoi cultures. The phase appears to be the result of a fusion of indigenous and foreign elements which filtered into Japan independently of one another over a long period of time. The foreign elements do not appear to have entered Japan as a block and thus the fusion represented by the phase must have taken place in Japan.

Available evidence does not link the origins of the Itazuke phase to any particular foreign area nor does it rule out the possibility that influences may have stemmed from a number of areas. The data also suggest that the earliest Yayoi cultures were not entirely different from nor necessarily vastly superior to existing Jomon cultures although the subsequent Yayoi spread was to prove a rapid process.

The evidence of physical anthropology suggests that there were physical changes in the Japanese population during the Yayoi period. The full importance and cause of these changes have, however, been variously interpreted and support can be found for almost any archaeological conclusion. Good evidence for any massive immigration into Japan at this time is lacking, and it seems safest to follow the conclusion of the many Japanese archaeologists who believe there was considerable continuity between Yayoi and Jomon populations.

Most Japanese archaeologists date Early Yayoi from about 400 to 100 B.C. The Itazuke phase accounts for perhaps the first half of this span. The latter half saw the rapid spread of the Yayoi complex as far east as the western Tokai district of central Honshu. The cultural complex that spread eastward is composed of ceramics (Ongagawa complex) derived from material like that associated with the Itazuke phase, the characteristic Yayoi polished stone tools which also appeared at that time, and sites which indicate either primitive rice agriculture or continued hunting and gathering activities. Evidence indicates that Ongagawa pottery (fig. 5.6) and the remainder of the Yayoi complex was carried into western Honshu by groups that subsequently mixed with the indigenous cultures.

Because many low-lying Early Yayoi sites have been buried in constantly moist alluvium, there is preservation of organic materials, and thus we have a good picture of the cultural inventory of the phase. Ceramically the sites are all very similar, and their lithic assemblages are also uniform and basically similar to the material described from Itazuke. The most characteristic stone tool from all interior Early Yayoi sites is the double perforated semi-lunar *ishibocho* sickle. Preserved in the wet levels of many sites is a sophisticated wooden tool industry of mortars, hoes, rakes, forks, and shovels. Baskets and other perishables were also recovered from the Karako site. Iron tools are very rare in Early Yayoi sites, but they are by no means unknown. As yet no evidence of artificially constructed or controlled wet rice fields has ever been

Figure 5.6. Ongagawa ware from the Nishishiga site (Sugihara, 1961, by permission).

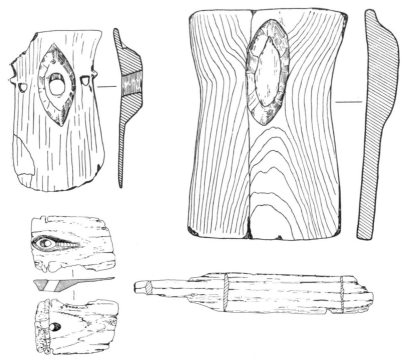

Figure 5.7. Yayoi wooden hoes and paddle-like implement (not to scale) (Sugihara, 1961, by permission).

linked to the Early Yayoi period. It appears that rice was still sown in natural swamps and bogs. Since it would seem unlikely that transplanting of young rice plants or careful preparation of fields could have been carried out in natural swamps, these operations were probably not characteristic of Early Yayoi agriculture. Harvesting is believed to have been accomplished with the *ishibocho* sickle. This implement was apparently tied to the hand by a cord passed through the two holes drilled near the dulled edge and was used to remove rice heads one at a time — a technique reminiscent of rice harvesting methods among many modern Southeast Asian groups. Cultivation of this type in uncontrolled swamps must not have been very productive since, as was noted earlier, there is no evidence of a significant increase in population during the Early Yayoi period. We must not assume, however, that the cultivation techniques of this time were undeveloped. It has been pointed out that the rapid spread of the pattern and the regularity of the tools associated with it indicate that the techniques were well-defined and established even before they appeared in Japan.

The Middle Yayoi stage (100 B.C.–100 A.D.) is marked by the first

significant appearance of continental bronze goods, the first glass ornaments, and regularized — perhaps mass produced — stone tools. Jar burials,
known during Early Yayoi times, are very typical of Middle Yayoi in western
Japan (fig. 5.8). More important than any of these markers were technical
advances made during the period which led to the rapid spread of agricultural
communities and development of even larger social institutions.

At the beginning of the Middle Yayoi stage there was both a rapid increase in the number of sites and in their areal distribution — an increase that
has been termed explosive. The biggest settlements continued to be located in
low alluvial areas although they were significantly larger than Early Yayoi
sites in the same areas. Technical advances also enabled utilization of narrow
mountain valleys and basins so that agricultural communities were able to
spread into these environments. This is also the period when agriculture and
the remainder of the Yayoi complex was being carried into eastern Honshu.
No doubt both of these movements are related. Although the new agricultural
techniques may have come about as a result of foreign influence into Japan —
and continued and close contact between Japan and Korea is very apparent at
this time — some Japanese archaeologists believe that the advances which
allowed for later Yayoi developments — water controls, adapted strains of
rice, and increased availability of iron tools — were developed from features
already present in Japan during Early Yayoi times.

Figure 5.8. Jar burials from the Kiridoshi site (Sugihara, 1961, by permission).

There are a great many later Yayoi sites situated on plateaus or ridges overlooking narrow mountain valleys. The artifact assemblages from such sites reflect agricultural activities, and most authors believe that they were small communities based on wet-rice agriculture, which was carried out in the adjoining valleys. If this interpretation is correct an elaborate water control system would have been required to make wet fields in such sloping valley locations. It also appears that dry upland agriculture was also practiced during later Yayoi times. This possibility has been suggested for sites in the uplands of Kumamoto prefecture, and such dry field crops as soy beans, red beans, rice (both wet and dry varieties), peas, broad beans, and two varieties of millet have been reported from upland sites in Okayama prefecture.

The best-known agricultural village of the Yayoi era is the Toro site, which is located near the southern coast of the Shizuoka plain, south of the modern city of Shizuoka. Excavations at the site have been nearly continuous for the past twenty-five years and have revealed the remains of a late Middle and Late Yayoi agricultural community along with the paddy fields which were associated with it (fig. 5.10).

Due to the excellent preservation at Toro, we have a good picture of the technology and economy of later Yayoi life. The elaborate wood tool industry shows that skillful wood working was characteristic of this time (fig. 5.11). The evidence suggests that iron was an available but scarce and valuable commodity even in later Yayoi times, so that scraps and broken tools were re-used and not readily discarded. This would explain the scarcity of iron recovered from Yayoi sites. The Toro community, with its elaborate agricultural technology featuring regularized special tools and transplanting of young rice plants into irrigated fields, shows all the basic features of historic Japanese farming. That technology therefore appears to date from the later half of the Yayoi era.

Thus the picture to be drawn from specific later Yayoi sites suggests that well-ordered, homogeneous farming villages were the main basis of society. At the same time there are indications of larger economic and political institutions which were also characteristic of this period. Most of the evidence for larger social institutions in later Yayoi society comes from studies made on the distribution of sites and of various goods and artifacts. These studies show that communities were linked to one another in various ways for a variety of purposes. New types of burial elaboration which appeared in some areas at this time also attest social changes. And finally, valuable information is also contained in Chinese historical records that refer to Japan in the Yayoi period. All these lines of evidence indicate that later Yayoi society was as varied and as regionally diverse as the artifact or ceramic assemblages of this time. It appears that different types of institutions were found in different areas and that some areas were socially far more complex than others.

Figure 5.9. Later Yayoi two-piece pedestal cooking pot (courtesy of Kurashiki Archaeological Museum and T. Makabe).

Figure 5.10. House floor from the Toro site (courtesy of S. Sugihara).

Given the nature of paddy-field rice agriculture, site distribution alone strongly suggests that organization above the level of the individual village was a feature of later Yayoi times. Communities located along valleys and other groups of communities that shared a common water source probably must have had an organization whereby they could coordinate their efforts at controlling and using their water supply. To Japanese archaeologists this sort of relationship was the most basic social elaboration of later Yayoi times and was probably present locally throughout much of Japan, although ethnographic analogy in various parts of the world would suggest that such organization need not have been very complex or powerful.

Aside from this sort of technical link, it appears that some later Yayoi communities specialized in the production and trading of specific commodities.

Most reviews of the Yayoi era place great stress on bronze goods, and it is true that these are quite striking and the most artistic of all Yayoi remains. In actual fact, however, little is known of their significance in Yayoi society and history. As we have seen, agricultural and wood-working tools continued to be made of iron, stone, or wood throughout the Yayoi period. Bronze does not appear to have been used for "technomic" artifacts. Instead it appears that most bronzes were socio-ideo-technic artifacts. Thus their full and true function is still a mystery, although there has been a great deal of speculation on this subject. It appears that there were several production centers for bronze

Figure 5.11. Wooden bowls, clogs, fire drill hearths, hoes, and spading forks from the Toro site (not to scale) (courtesy of S. Sugihara).

Figure 5.12. Yayoi bronze spear points (*Kokogaku Syukan*, vol. 4, no. 2).

Figure 5.13. Bronze "bell" (Sugihara, 1961, by permission).

weapons in western Japan and that, even for widely traded types, tastes or requirements of various localities were not uniform (fig. 5.12).

Besides weapons, the other major category of Yayoi bronzes is called "bells," although they are very problematical objects (fig. 5.13). Unlike Yayoi weapons, which often have foreign prototypes, these bells (*dotaku*) appear to be completely indigenous Japanese products. Similar bells are not known from the mainland, and in Japan they are concentrated in the Kinki district, not in an area adjacent to the continent. Mirrors, another category, are considerably scarcer than either bells or weapons. These are unmistakably imported objects made in China in the last century B.C. (fig. 5.14). Locally produced mirrors seem to have appeared only during the subsequent Kofun period. Together these bronze goods provide many implications about Yayoi society and economy. First, it is certain that there was inter-community trade in bronzes either brought from the continent or made at one of the few production centers in Japan. Distribution studies show that this trade was far-reaching, with goods from the continent or Kyushu being carried as far eastward as present-day Nagoya. Distribution studies also suggest that the bronze requirements of the Kinki district were different from those of northern Kyushu and the area around the western end of the Inland Sea. Since bronzes

Figure 5.14. Bronze mirror (Han) from the Mitsunagata site (Sugihara, 1961, by permission).

were apparently for ceremonial use, this difference suggests that these areas had different social or religious organizations. Early Chinese records which refer to later Yayoi Japan indicate that small "states" and social stratification were present at least in northern Kyushu by this time.

The earliest mention of Japan in the Chinese chronicles is the record of an envoy from the state of Nu — thought to have been located in northern Kyushu — who visited the Han court in 57 A.D. This record supports the archaeologically drawn conclusion that by the Middle Yayoi stage there was frequent intercourse between Kyushu and the continent.

In summary, during later Yayoi times well-ordered agricultural communities based on sophisticated irrigated rice farming were typical of even mountainous sections of western Japan. These communities were tied together in a variety of ways to form larger social units. The most basic links were based on trade relations or the technical requirements of irrigation. Large areas seem to have shared religious cults, and, at least in northern Kyushu, stratified political states were formed.

In the Final Jomon period, the area east of the Tokai was the heartland of the Kamegaoka complex. This vigorous development linked the entire area together at the end of the Jomon era so that even if the complex had become "stagnant" by Early Yayoi times, the Jomon cultures of eastern Honshu were still the most energetic ones met by the spread of the Yayoi cultural complex. Thus it is not surprising that this complex incorporated many elements from the Jomon tradition as it spread into this area. We saw that the initial spread of the Yayoi complex in western Japan, as marked by Ongagawa pottery, was rapid and incorporated little from the pre-existing cultures of the area. The spread was halted about 200 B.C. when it reached the Tokai. The first evidence of the continued spread of Yayoi cultures is seen about one hundred years later (i.e., early in the Middle Yayoi stage). Contact Yayoi sites in southern Tohoku are rare, suggesting that populations were small, and almost all of the reported sites are shell middens. This would indicate that rice agricultural techniques had been added to the pre-existing gathering economy, which was probably still dominant. In this regard it is significant that iron was used for hunting implements. Clearly the phase was not agricultural in the same sense as later Yayoi cultures of western Japan were. The evidence would suggest that the contact phase of southern Tohoku is in many respects similar to the Itazuke phase of Kyushu. Perhaps they can both be viewed as basically indigenous (Jomon) cultures altered by the addition of elements from a spreading or at least an advanced neighbor. It would further appear that the first elements adopted in both cases were much the same: metal tools, weaving, and burial elaboration. Of course, rice agriculture was also among the first elements adopted, but in both cases it was grafted on to earlier occupations to form a mixed economic pattern which did not give rise to large habitation sites. During the period from about 75–300 A.D. eastern Honshu achieved a greater level of cultural homogeneity and the Yayoi cultural complex completed its spread by reaching the northern tip of the island. This is also the time during which the cultures of eastern Honshu clearly broke with the Jomon tradition and formed a distinct cultural pattern based on the Yayoi complex.

To summarize, the origins of the Yayoi era seem clearly linked to an intrusion of cultural patterns into Japan. What we have called the Itazuke phase appears to represent a culture which includes at least three major patterns not to be drawn from the Jomon tradition: iron, weaving, and rice agriculture. Examination of the phase shows, however, that these elements formed only a part of a well-integrated culture that clearly owed much to preceding local cultures. Furthermore, the new elements themselves did not appear to be entirely original with the Itazuke phase. Instead it appears that they filtered into Kyushu independent of one another throughout the Final Jomon period. Thus both the Itazuke phase and the Yayoi tradition appear to have been "made in Japan." The precise source of the foreign elements remains unknown, and the possibility still remains open that two or more areas contributed to the formation of the first Yayoi culture. The link between Kyushu and the rest of the world during the earlier part of Yayoi times was, at any rate, tenuous indeed. Economically the Itazuke phase may not have been far removed from the Jomon tradition of hunting and gathering. The present evidence suggests that sedentary life was not yet well developed and that farming was only a part-time and perhaps seasonal pursuit.

The eastward spread of the Yayoi cultural complex was so rapid that it must have been associated at least in part with a movement of people. This rapid spread clearly shows that even the primitive Early Yayoi farming technique was superior to the indigenous economies. Perhaps the road had been cleared for the Yayoi spread by experimentation with domestic crops during the Final Jomon period.

After about 50 B.C. the Yayoi cultures of western Japan were clearly in fairly close and regular contact with the continent. At this time and subsequently the major continental contact was via Korea. This period saw the rapid development of several aspects of Yayoi life. It is tempting to link these developments to an outside stimulus, but in doing so the possibility of indigenous developments in agriculture and society must not be forgotten. Whatever its source, the economic pattern which characterizes historic Japan dates from this period. The social structures associated with Japanese rice agriculture must also have been developing at this time. In the shadow of Han China it seems impossible to view the political developments of later Yayoi times as indigenous. By the end of the Yayoi period, however, fairly sophisticated political institutions — at least of the "chiefdom" magnitude — were present in Japan. Thus it seems unnecessary to call on further massive intrusion to explain the developments of the subsequent Kofun period.

As the Yayoi cultural complex spread into eastern Japan it became closely associated with many Jomon traits. As a result, the Yayoi cultures of the area bear a striking similarity to the Itazuke phase. At first only the basics of the Yayoi complex were introduced to eastern Japan, and Jomon economic patterns were abandoned only very slowly. With time, all of Honshu had a Yayoi cast although throughout the Yayoi period eastern Honshu was marginal to the western Yayoi heartland.

The fourth to seventh centuries A.D. in Japan are assigned to the Kofun or Tomb period. It was during this time that Japan passed from prehistory to the historically known civilization of the Asuka and Nara periods. In many respects the Kofun period is protohistoric since our knowledge of the time does not rest solely on archaeological evidence. A fairly large number of historical sources, both from the continent and from within Japan itself, refer to this period and shed considerable light on the social and historical developments that ultimately resulted in historic Japanese civilization. The period is also marked by the appearance of large, conspicuous, and richly outfitted burial mounds which have been intensively studied by archaeologists. The archaeological material dating from this period includes various types of artifacts which reveal both the internal social developments taking place within Japan itself and the growing external contacts between Japan and the continent. However, in spite of all these lines of evidence, it is still very difficult to present a unified and balanced picture of the life and cultural developments of the period. The historical sources are often confusing and incomplete, leaving many questions unanswered. The data of archaeology supplement these records and no doubt could be further used to fill in the voids that still exist. As in other parts of the world, however, monumental architecture, in the form of the burial mounds which give the period its name, has attracted the primary attention of Kofun specialists. Comparatively few habitation sites are known from the period and published reports on remains of this type are for the most part the result of recent salvage projects made in advance of urban expansion. Furthermore, analysis of Kofun age remains has most often been motivated by aesthetic concerns, so that unusually fine examples have been stressed to the exclusion of the mass of more commonplace finds.

For all of these reasons it is very difficult to link archaeological findings with known historical developments of the Kofun period. Nor can the archaeological data available be presented in terms of well-characterized cultural phases.

Whereas Jomon and Yayoi archaeologists have usually built their cultural reconstructions and regional sequences around successions of pottery complexes, Kofun specialists have instead emphasized chronologies and periodization based on changes in tombs and their furnishings. The habitation sites from this period are poorly reported; those best known appear to date from fairly late in the period and thus offer a poor basis for a chronological sequence. The domestic pottery and artifacts made during the period are also not useful chronological markers. The Haji domestic pottery, for example, persists with scant regional or temporal variation from the end of the Yayoi period until the Heian period. It is thus quite understandable that attempts to establish cultural chronology for the period have relied on material recovered from tombs.

There are, however, two major limitations to the use of any of the Kofun chronologies which have been based on funeral remains. First, they are not of general utility since it is difficult to link domestic remains to them. Second, even tomb chronologies are of limited validity since there are no clear horizon markers with which to divide the period. Thus archaeological subdivisions of the Kofun period cannot be given precise definition. For a general review of the culture historical developments of the period, two subperiods seem most useful. Early Kofun saw the appearance of mound tombs and the introduction of some new foreign materials, but appears basically to represent an extensive and indigenous elaboration of Yayoi culture. Later, midway through the fifth century, the results of Japan's growing foreign involvements became increasingly apparent and are the major characteristic of Late Kofun times.

Mound tombs, the most common archaeological remains of the Kofun period, are distributed from southern Kyushu to southern Tohoku, and although their original number will never be known, it must have been at least on the order of ten thousand. Archaeologically, the beginning of the Kofun period dates from the appearance of these burial mounds which give the period its name. In fact, however, the origin of the mounds and the exact date and place of their appearance is not precisely known, so that the initial date of 300 A.D. usually assigned to Kofun is quite arbitrary. The major basis of absolute chronology is the cross dating of continental imports contained in the tombs as grave goods, the most important of which in Early Kofun times are bronze mirrors.

Tombs dating from the fourth century are found from Kyushu to Kanto but, as in subsequent periods, the center of tomb construction was in the Kinki district, the vicinity of modern Kyoto-Osaka. Again as in subsequent tomb-building periods, a variety of types of tombs are typical of Early Kofun times. Characteristically, tombs were built singly in hilly locations away from areas suitable for agriculture. This suggests that flat land was too valuable to be used for burial. Most of these early tombs have a round ground plan and, though by now highly eroded, were built in the shape of a flat-topped cone. A relatively few early tombs had a small square or trapezoidal section built on one side of a round conoid mound. These mounds thus have a "key-hole" shape, and this type persists throughout the entire Kofun period. The significance of such tombs is not known. Precise foreign parallels for the form are lacking, although some authors have looked to certain aspects of Chinese funeral ritual and ceremonialism for possible prototypes. It is also suggested, again without supporting evidence, that the square annex was originally intended as a platform for funeral rites. This explanation is not implausible since we have many documentary records indicating that death and burial at this time were accompanied by considerable ritual activity. There is no evidence to suggest that permanent or substantial temporary structures were built atop these square annexes.

Inside Early Kofun tombs, the body of the buried person and the associated grave goods were most often placed in a chamber of roughly coursed stone slabs. These chambers were built on or near the original ground level at the base of the mound, but because they were built and entered from the top they are called ''vertical stone chambers.'' They were either built on the ground surface and subsequently covered with the earthen fill of the mound or they were made by lining with stones the sides of a trench cut into the half-completed mound. The stones used were most commonly only very roughly shaped, if at all. Fairly small slabs of naturally bedded stone such as andesite or limestone were preferred for the walls of these early burial chambers. The floor of the chamber was either unfinished earth or paved with flat stone slabs. The ceiling or top, which was the final addition to a chamber, was usually made of very large flat slabs of stone which straddled the side walls.

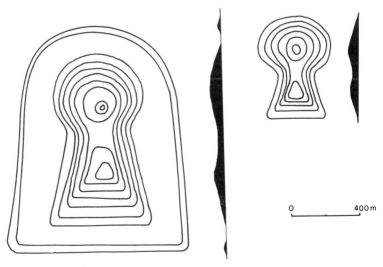

Figure 5.15. Contour plans and profiles of typical ''key-hole'' burial mounds (drawing by Peter Bleed).

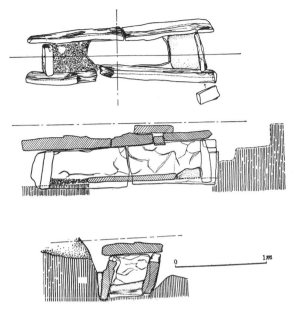

Figure 5 16 Early Kofun burial chamber — plan, horizontal profile, and cross section — from Mokuroji (after Otsuka and Kobayashi).

This construction technique required that the chambers be quite narrow, and their usual width is rarely more than one meter. Length, on the other hand, was more variable, and vertical chambers more than eight meters long are not unusual. The extra space provided by the long chambers was filled with grave goods.

The body of the person buried in Early Kofun mounds was usually placed in a wood or stone coffin. Wood coffins were made by splitting and hollowing out the halves of a single large tree trunk. The outside of the coffin was thus cylindrical. Stone coffins typical of Early Kofun times are also made of two hollowed sections which, when fitted together, form a cylinder. They thus appear to be copies of wooden prototypes. Beside the vertical stone chambered tombs with cylindrical coffins, other burial modes occasionally met with in Early Kofun period mounds include burial in a simple coffin set in an unlined trench, burial with or without a coffin in a rectangular cist of vertically set stone slabs, and burial in a vertical chamber without a coffin.

A characteristic and famous feature of the Kofun period, the haniwa figures, originated during Early Kofun times and are commonly associated with the burial mounds. Haniwa are hollow cylindrical clay sculptures. During Later Kofun times they assumed very famous zoomorphic and anthropomorphic shapes. The figurines which date from Early Kofun, however, are nearly always either simple problematical cylindrical forms, or they protray hand tools, houses, and other inanimate objects. Technically, the haniwa of both subperiods are identical, being hand modeled of unglazed clay. Technologically they are clearly an outgrowth of the domestic Haji pottery tradition of the Kofun period. In terms of surface finish, construction, and firing techniques, and even general shape, they are very similar to the domestic pottery of the period. Such figurines appear to have been a part of the Kofun burial complex from its very inception. Typically the figurines, if present, were placed in a closely spaced row along the basal edge of a mound. Sometimes a second or even third concentric row of haniwa figurines was also placed around a mound at approximately mid-height. The origin and significance of haniwa figurines remain unsolved problems. Various sorts of tomb figurines are typical of much of East Asia, and so it is commonly suggested that haniwa figurines represent a foreign trait which was introduced into Japan early in the Kofun period. Specific parallels for the peculiarities of the Japanese figurines are, however, unknown on the continent. Recorded in the *Nihon Shoki* is a myth — in no way verified by archaeology — which suggests that anthropomorphic haniwa were made and used to replace living attendants that had at one time been sacrificed when their master died. There is no evidence that retainer burial was ever practiced in Japan and the myth also fails to explain the significance of the haniwa portraying inanimate objects, which predate the appearance of anthropomorphic styles.

Figure 5.17. Reconstruction of typical burial mound with haniwa in position (original sketch by R. K. Beardsley; by permission of the artist and *Journal of Asian Studies*).

Present in early Kofun tombs are several characteristic types of burial wealth that set this subperiod apart from the following one. Bronze mirrors have already been mentioned. Their use as grave goods represents the persistence of a Yayoi pattern and indicates, of course, continued contact with China and other continental cultures. An important innovation of Early Kofun times is the appearance of native Japanese copies of continental prototypes. These appear during the fourth century and, although not always of the best workmanship, very early assume distinctive Japanese qualities.

The grave goods most characteristic of Early Kofun are beautifully carved stone or glass ornaments. The most numerous category of the former are beads which are present in great numbers — up to ten thousand — in some graves. The commonest shapes are spherical, cylindrical, and facetted, but the most famous are the so-called "comma-shaped" beads, or *magatama* (fig. 5.18). The latter, together with the sword and the mirror, formed part of the sacred imperial regalia mentioned in early historical records and thus may well have had both religious and decorative significance. Beads were carved of clear and colored glass and of quartz, green jasper, jadeite, and steatite. The regularity and high quality workmanship exhibited by the beads suggests that they were made by highly trained specialists. Other large carved stone ornaments typically associated with early mound burials are called bracelets although their true function is unknown. These are either circular or trapezoidal in plan and have a central round or ovoid hole (fig. 5.19).

Weapons are regularly met with in Early Kofun tombs although the range of types known from this time does not compare with the diversity seen in later times. Bronze weapons of the sort found in some Yayoi burials are not typical of Early Kofun. Rather, practical iron weapons are the rule. Included in this category are narrow socketed spears which are not too dissimilar in shape from Yayoi bronze spears. Far more common than spears are long

Figure 5.18. *Magatama* beads (courtesy of Tokyo National Museum, by permission).

Figure 5.19. Stone bracelets (not to scale) (courtesy of Japanese Department of Culture, Ministry of Education, and T. Kobayashi).

straight iron swords. These are very similar to Han Chinese swords in that they are single edged and have a permanently affixed hilt which ends in a simple ring pommel. They were not highly decorated, although they were sometimes deposited in burials in very large numbers — commonly twenty or more. It would appear that the technical patterns of later Japanese swords — laminated steel blade, edge tempering, as well as the basic canons of sword fittings and mounts — were established at this time. Bronze arrowheads are a third weapon type which is commonly found in Early Kofun tombs. Body armor is rare in the earliest Kofun burials and that which does date from the subperiod is not of the design quality of subsequent Kofun armor. The few earliest examples known are all poorly preserved, apparently because they consisted of small squares of iron which were sewn on a cloth or leather backing.

There is enough saddlery contained in Early Kofun tombs to show that the horse was present in Japan and was a part of the Early Kofun military complex, but since this material is quite limited the importance of the horse may not have been great.

The last category of grave goods common in Early Kofun tombs consists of iron tools. In fact, by far the largest number of iron tools known from this time have been recovered from tombs rather than habitation sites. All indications are, however, that the tools used as grave goods were identical to the hand tools in daily use during the fourth century. It has been suggested that these tools were included in graves as ritual objects, and since historical sources do indicate that the early emperors and other leaders performed fertility rituals with the aid of utilitarian objects, this interpretation seems plausible. Quite aside from the supposed ritual function, the fact that iron tools are so much more common in tombs than in habitation sites would indicate that iron was still a relatively rare commodity quite worthy of inclusion as burial treasure. Tools used as burial wealth include socketed axes and adzes, chisels and hoes, one-piece handled adzes, awls, and a variety of items that appear to be fishing equipment: hooks, gaffs, spears, and harpoons.

The Early Kofun tombs represent a sizable amount of labor and the quantity of goods included in some of the graves reflects considerable wealth. Though not perhaps comparable to the wealth of some Han Chinese or later Japanese burials, still the labor and treasure represented in these Early Kofun tombs is certainly much greater than that of typical Yayoi "elite" burials and would thus appear to be a general reflection of social developments which were taking place in Japan at this time.

Since mound burial appears to be such an important part of the culture of Early Kofun times, the question of its origins is basic to an understanding of the roots of protohistoric Japanese culture. In the past, East Asian archaeology has been dominated by diffusionists, and majority opinion has tended to link the origin of the Japanese burial complex with similar patterns in the North China-Korea area. There are, to be sure, many similarities between Early Kofun burial practices and burial patterns in other parts of Asia. There have even been vague suggestions that the Kofun complex is related to and derived from the mound burials of Inner Asia. Mound burial is, of course, typical of much of the steppe region, but the distribution of that pattern is for the most part limited to the region west of the Altai mountains so that it seems an unlikely source for the Japanese mounds. The mound and cist burials common in the North China area offer a more likely progenitor for the Japanese tombs although they are still so poorly known that it is very difficult to demonstrate any link between these areas. Burial mounds appeared in China itself as early as the Eastern Chou period and attendant sacrifice (which the early Japanese saw as the origin of haniwa figurines) is a prominent Shang pattern. Thus many elements of the Kofun burial complex were present in China before the Kofun period. In Korea, Japan's closest neighbor, "dolmens" are a very common — though poorly dated — feature of the archaeological landscape. All of the Korean dolmens have been assigned to the "Bronze Age," but this tells us little about their precise time placement. Two basic types of dolmens have been identified in Korea. Both of these are widely distributed throughout the country although they are called "northern" and "southern" types. The "northern" type, which is thought to be the older of the two, resembles a table with a large flat capstone resting on a few equally large supports. This type of dolmen has no parallels among the Early Kofun tombs of Japan. The "southern" type, which has been loosely linked to the period A.D. 1 to A.D. 400, includes elements associated with both Yayoi and Kofun burials. The main similarity between these dolmens and early Japanese tombs is the use of vertical stone slab burial chambers. Aside from this there are many differences between the two. All of this evidence suggests that the development of mound burial was a widely dispersed phenomenon in East Asia, with several areas adapting a basic pattern which itself may have been the product of diverse elements. Japan appears to have been one area taking part in and interacting with others in this development. With this approach we need not search for foreign prototypes and sources for all the unique aspects of the Japanese tomb complex: the "keyhole-shaped" mounds, clay haniwa, distinctive coffins, and the unique grave goods. Instead, the complex can be viewed as a unique Japanese phenomenon developed in Japan under varying stimuli. As archaeology on the continent develops it may be possible to sort out some of these varied stimuli more precisely.

The presently available evidence indicates that one of the major influences on the Early Kofun burial complex came from preceding Late Yayoi burial practices which, of course, may themselves be ultimately of foreign origin. The most characteristic form of elite burial of the Late Yayoi period is in a double jar like the mass of other burials, but accompanied by grave goods in the form of bronze mirrors or weapons. Certain Early Kofun polished stone objects have Yayoi parallels and slab stone cist burials are also typical of both periods. There are even Late Yayoi burials associated with low mound structures which in some ways appear to be transitional between Yayoi and Kofun style graves. Thus at the very least, if mound burial was introduced into Japan early in the Kofun period, the idea of elaborate burial with major grave goods for the socially elite was a well-established pattern before that time. Since it is clear that "dolmen" or mound burial was a widespread pattern in East Asia at about the time of the advent of the Kofun period, and since Japan was at this time clearly in close contact with continental Asia, the Kofun burial complex must be related to a non-Japanese source. It is important, however, not to overlook the similarities and continuities — both general and specific — that exist between Early Kofun and preceding Yayoi burial practices.

As stated earlier, the domestic side of Early Kofun culture is very poorly known since so few habitation sites of the period have been adequately studied. Our best information concerns the domestic Haji pottery of the time (fig. 5.20). Studies indicate that the basic domestic ceramic industry of the Kofun period has its technological roots in the Yayoi period and that once established in Early Kofun times, it did not undergo significant change until well into the historic period. The most striking features of the early Haji pottery complex are its homogeneity throughout western Japan and its rapid spread throughout its distribution. It has been suggested that the spread of Haji pottery through its full range was completed by the mid-fourth century, and that this rapid spread was linked to the expanding political unity of the Yamato state. The monotonous uniformity of the ware is believed by many to indicate that it was produced by a specialized group of potters.

Figure 5.20. Haji ware from Nakada site (courtesy of Atsuko Okada).

Remains of Early Kofun domestic architecture are rare indeed. Strangely, most of the houses known from this time are from the then marginal Kanto district. It is possible that this "frontier" region was less advanced than the Kinki district, the available evidence suggesting that there was at this time little change or improvement over Late Yayoi living conditions. Agricultural villages were still apparently relatively small. They were composed of shallow square pit dwellings about five meters on a side with four central support posts and a central pit hearth. At sites such as Goryo in Saitama prefecture remains of sixteen or more dwellings dating from this period have been found but all of these were clearly not occupied at the same time. At other sites, such as Nakada in western Tokyo, which contain large numbers of later Kofun house remains, only a very few Early houses have been found. This suggests that population levels were low at the beginning of the protohistoric period. With the limited data available, however, it seems unwise to speculate further about the society of the period.

Early Kofun-period haniwa which portray houses suggest that there were several more types of domestic structures and considerably more complexity in that area than has been revealed by archaeological research. Haniwa representations of houses have been found at several Early Kofun sites (fig. 5.21). They appear to represent substantial, even massive, rectangular struc-

Figure 5.21. Early Kofun house haniwa from Akabori (after Goto).

tures built of planks and topped with thick gabled and hip and gabled thatched roofs. A variety of floor plans are shown and some appear to represent pile structures. The fact that haniwa houses were associated with graves of the socially elite suggests that they represent the homes of these same people. The masses probably lived in pit houses like those mentioned above.

Very little is known about the domestic technology and economic basis of Early Kofun times. Iron seems to have been used primarily for the sharp working edges of tools that were otherwise made entirely of wood. The technique of "shoeing" the tips of shovels, hoes, plows, and wood-working tools was present in Japan by Late Yayoi times. In fact, most Early Kofun iron tools are identical to forms known from the Yayoi period and are generally less sophisticated than later protohistoric tools.

In summary, the most striking advance of the Early Kofun subperiod was the appearance of a new elite burial complex featuring construction of mounds and rich burial wealth. This complex seems to have been strongly influenced by non-Japanese patterns, but it also shows continuity with preceding Japanese burial patterns. The elaborations which were introduced must have fallen on fertile soil, for internal Japanese social developments seem to have given rise, by this time, to a stratified society. Social stratification, seen archaeologically in burial practices, reached new heights but again seems in no way to represent a break with Yayoi developments. Trade with the continent dates from the Yayoi period. Technologically and economically the limited evidence that is available shows no improvement or change in the sophisticated wet-rice agriculture which had already been developed in Japan during Yayoi times. Indeed no basic improvements have been made in these patterns until very recently. Thus, on the whole, Early Kofun may be viewed as a cultural extension and indigenous elaboration of Yayoi culture which was receiving cultural stimuli from abroad, to a greater extent than preceding cultures, but less than its successors.

The Late Kofun subperiod started in the mid-fifth century and ended as an archaeological period in the Yamato area early in the seventh century. No doubt certain elements associated with the period persisted sometime longer in outlying areas. By this time Japan had been in close contact — and conflict — with several Korean and Chinese governments for more than a hundred years, and the material effects of this foreign contact were becoming increasingly and strikingly apparent. Archaeologically this period is marked by a rapid increase of grave goods showing strong foreign influences. Several new types appear in the burial mounds of this period, and nearly all of the goods have a new "foreign" appearance. Historically, it is known that this was a period of political development, with the central court increasing in both size and politi cal power. These developments are reflected archaeologically in increases in the number and areal distribution of burial mounds. Archaeological data on the domestic culture and technology of the period are again not as complete as they might be, but the evidence seems to indicate that the lives of the great masses of people remained much as they had been during Early Kofun times. On this level, any changes seem to have been relatively minor.

No new burial mound forms are associated with Late Kofun. Again, the most striking mounds are "key-hole" shaped. Typically, however, the later key-hole mounds are surrounded by systems of moats and embankments. Several of these tombs are also literally colossal in size, with mounds of more than four hundred meters in length not being unusual. Conical round and pyramidal square-based mounds are also characteristic of the Late Kofun period. Often these forms were built as the smaller auxiliaries around the huge key-hole mounds. Whereas Early tombs had been built singly in remote or hilly situations, Late period tombs were usually constructed on fertile level land. The tendency to build mounds in groups was another major development in Late Kofun times. Often the groups were composed of a huge central mound which was surrounded by a scatter of variously shaped smaller mounds. The social significance of these groups of mounds is not known. The general haphazard layout of most of them would indicate that they were not built according to a unified plan, and there is no positive evidence to suggest that the groups reflect specific social units. Perhaps the groups of mounds merely indicate that certain areas were set aside and viewed as burial areas. The increased number of mounds and the variety of sizes and opulence they exhibit would appear to be a reflection of the growth of administrative and political bodies. Whereas only the local aristocratic leaders rated mound burial during the Early Kofun period, the number of individuals worthy of such treatment in Late Kofun times was greatly increased.

Vertical stone burial chambers of Early Kofun style were made in Late Kofun times, but the most striking innovation of the later burial complex was the appearance of the so-called horizontal burial chambers. Unlike the older forms, these chambers were made with the access on one of the side walls rather than through the top. They are thus much more like an actual room and were, in fact, usually built like a free-standing structure. It appears that the earliest of the horizontal chambered tombs are found in Kyushu and that they spread from there to central Honshu. The earliest forms were typically built of roughly coursed undressed slabs of stone — the same technique used in the construction of the older vertical chambers. The very famous horizontal chambers of semi-dressed blocks or even of huge well-dressed ''megalithic'' blocks are a feature of the seventh century. They are found from northern Kyushu to central Honshu and can be viewed as the ultimate elaboration of the Kofun-period burial complex. Painted tombs typical of the later Kofun period of Kyushu are another type of late elaboration of the complex.

Coffins were not universally used with horizontal chambered tombs. Sometimes the body was placed in the chamber either uncovered or covered only with a perishable wrap. Most of the coffins that were used during this period were derived from the ''split log'' stone coffins of the preceding period. In general, although the Late Kofun period saw significant elaboration in burial architecture, it was for the most part elaboration of pre-existing Japanese traits.

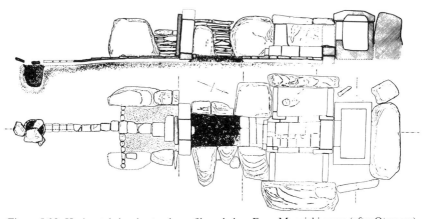

Figure 5.22. Horizontal chamber tomb: profile and plan. From Mannichi-yama (after Otomasu).

Cyclindrical modeled clay haniwa figurines are another trait that survived into Late Kofun times. In place of the house- and utensil-shaped haniwa that surrounded Early Kofun tombs, Late tombs are typically associated with zoomorphic or anthropomorphic figurines (figs. 5.23, 5.24). These figures were commonly placed in rows both around the mounds and on the embankments that surrounded some of them. In construction and use they are identical to Early Kofun haniwa. Zoomorphic figurines were especially popular during the fifth and sixth centuries. Nearly all of the animals portrayed by the figurines — horses, dogs, oxen, boars, chickens, and ducks — would appear to have been economically important. Haniwa portraying monkeys, deer, and other wild animals are also known. Anthropomorphic haniwa appeared late in the fifth century and provide insights into the dress and culture of Late Kofun times. Stylistically all of the anthropomorphic haniwa are much alike, with blank, rather generalized faces. Their costumes and stances are, however, quite varied, and it would appear that a variety of social classes and occupational specialists are represented. Commoners are apparently represented by plainly dressed, smiling farmers, some of whom have what appear to be hoes tucked in their belts. Such court attendants as musicians, dancers, and falconers are also portrayed. Other men are much more elegantly turned out, with brimmed hats and side-opening or long double-breasted tunics secured by ties. Men also appear to have worn baggy trousers. Hair was worn in a variety of styles, and several males are shown wearing beards. Many haniwa figures, both male and female, have red painted designs on their faces. It has been proposed that these might represent tattooing, but recent analysis of the relevant documentary sources suggests that they are more likely painted cosmetics. A number of the males portrayed by haniwa are clad in armor and carry weapons. The armor, which appears to be identical to actual suits contained in contemporary tombs, consists of a plate cuirass reaching to the hips, a close-fitting helmet, and tied-on greaves. Some of the armed figures carry a bow and a protective arm brace, but nearly all males, even those without armor, carry a single long sword hung from the belt. Women wore the same kind of double-breasted tunic as the men, but below it they wore a skirt that left the lower leg exposed. Both sexes are commonly shown wearing such ornaments as round and *magatama* beads and stone bracelets. A few also appear to be carrying bronze mirrors suspended from their belts. The clothing, armor, and other aspects of the costumery of Late Kofun haniwa are often viewed as ''new'' elements which were introduced into Japan during the period. In fact, however, so little is known about the personal adornment of Early Kofun times that no firm comparison is possible. The ornaments shown on later figurines are essentially identical to those found in early tombs. Thus the major difference between the costumes of the two subperiods may be that we have a record only from the later.

Figure 5.23. Late Kofun zoomorphic and anthropomorphic haniwa (courtesy of Tokyo National Museum and Aikawa Museum).

Figure 5.24. Late Kofun warrior haniwa (courtesy Tenri Sankokan Museum).

Carved stone ornaments typically associated with Early Kofun burials are not a characteristic type of grave goods in the Late Period. In their place, the typical grave wealth in late burials is in the form of weapons or gold or gilt ornaments. Typically, all of the goods included in the graves of this period were very richly decorated, and this must be considered their basic characteristic. The most frequently encountered weapons are straight single edge swords. Until very late in the period, these swords appear to be elaborations of the ring-pommeled Han Chinese-style swords of Early times. Such swords were often deposited in tombs in large numbers; some tombs are known to have contained nearly a hundred. Toward the end of the period, new types of swords with cylindrical caps or large bulbous pommels appeared. Most of the Late Kofun swords were equipped with a stubby flat-sided blade that seems in every way functional. Socketed iron spearheads mounted on wooden poles are also common grave finds of the later period, as are long bows. The bows were of wood and wrapped with split bamboo or some other fiber. The ends were fitted with a metal tip, often the only part of the original that survives. Iron arrow points shaped like the earlier bronze ones are now the rule.

Body armor from Late tombs is much superior to the simple plate protection known from earlier burials. In the area outside the Yamato heartland, armor is commonly met with in all types and sizes of graves. In the Kinki district, however, armor has never been found in major key-hole-shaped mounds. Rather, it is invariably located in smaller auxiliary mounds situated near the larger ones. Large caches of other types of weapons are also commonly located in such small mounds. To many researchers, this evidence suggests that armor was not primarily the property of the highest levels of Late Kofun society. In outlying areas it was associated with the elite, but near the central court, armor appears to have been the property of a relatively lower class.

Horse equipment was a popular and conspicuous type of Late Kofun burial wealth indicating that the horse played an important role in the military organization of the time.

A major category of Late Kofun grave goods is Sue pottery, a high-fired, wheel-thrown ware that was present, though rare, during Early Kofun times (fig. 5.25). It is formally and technically so similar to the contemporary pottery of Silla and other Asian kingdoms that it must have been introduced into Japan. Because of the Korean affinities, the suddenness of its appearance, and its striking uniformity throughout Japan, and also because of the strongly corporate nature of the early potter's guilds, it is widely believed that the first Sue pottery was made by Koreans. Sue ware, whatever its source, was quickly adopted by the Japanese and incorporated into Japanese patterns. It was clearly a nonutilitarian ware, for it is rarely met with in habitation sites and is most common in graves.

Until recently it was commonly hypothesized that the establishment of the Japanese imperial household and other developments of the protohistoric

Figure 5.25. Sue ware from Yamahata 35 mound, Osaka (courtesy Higashi-Osaka City Museum).

period were the results of an invasion of Japan by continental groups. But historical research has led to the conclusion that a simple invasion theory is untenable, and many Japanese archaeologists now realize that such a view cannot adequately explain the archaeologically known complexities of the period. Still, since some respectable Japanese scholars do continue to find the theory useful and many English language summaries have accepted this general interpretation and tend to present a patently simplistic picture of the period, it is thus a view we must briefly consider.

The clearest presentation of this theory is offered by Namio Egami (1962), who hypothesizes that a militant pastoral tribe from northeastern Asia became the ruling class of Japan over the aborigines. Egami's view rests on linguistic, historical, and mythological research as well as on the data of archaeology. He and several other authors contend that there is a marked similarity between several later Kofun and continental traits. In this connection, mound and cist tombs, arms, and the decorative and artistic complexes seem especially important. Although parallels for these features can be found on the continent, they are sometimes far removed from Japan or not clearly ancestral to Japanese forms. Thus, for example, J. Edward Kidder points out painted tombs in the Yalu valley of Korea that parallel but post-date Japanese tombs. Others of the suggested parallels are of a very general nature and do not convincingly demonstrate cultural contact. And the parallels which are most often cited are drawn from a vast variety of continental complexes. As yet there are no known Asiatic cultures that resemble the later Kofun complex, and there are also any number of Kofun-period traits that are without foreign parallels and are instead unique to Japan. The invasion theory thus lacks convincing demonstration.

The number of adequately reported Late Kofun habitation sites is not great, but the domestic culture of this period is more completely known than that of earlier times. All of the well-reported habitation sites are in the Kanto or elsewhere in eastern Japan, and in most other areas the Haji ceramic industry is the only adequately known aspect of the domestic culture. It is thus impossible to describe the regional variation which might have existed between Late Kofun communities. The evidence which is available suggests that there may have been some slight regional variation at this time, but it does not appear to have been significant. The uniformity of Haji pottery from Kyushu to Tohoku is so great as to suggest cultural homogeneity throughout the region. The known village sites also bespeak broad uniformity, so that until there is evidence to the contrary, it seems safe to assume that local communities throughout western Japan were broadly similar and that the well-studied villages of the Kanto are representative of the communities of this period.

The best known Kofun-period village is the Nakada site, located in the western suburbs of Tokyo. This is a large site that was intensively occupied throughout Late Kofun times. The dwellings and other village refuse are distributed along the low natural knoll which parallels the Kawaguchi River. Behind the knoll is a low flat area which is today covered with wet-rice fields (and probably has been since the Yayoi period). Excavators stripped nearly all of the five-hundred-meter-long knoll and found the remains of 135 pit structures. Since the site had been occupied throughout and, indeed, subsequent to the Kofun period, the site plan was rather complex and confusing. It does not appear, however, that the structures of any given phase were arranged in an obvious pattern. Houses were scattered along the knoll facing either north toward the rice fields or south toward the river. Construction techniques were fairly uniform throughout the Late Kofun period. Nearly all houses were square in plan, ranging in size from four to eight meters on a side (sixteen square meters to sixty-four square meters). Each house was very carefully laid out and it has even been suggested that a standard *shaku* length measure (twenty-four centimeters) was used in planning and making the structures. A house floor was excavated to slightly below soil surface (less than fifty centimeters), and the walls were vertically set in wall trenches on the inside of the excavated portion. Four or six symmetrically spaced vertical posts supported the roof, but in spite of many attempts at reconstruction, the original form of the superstructure is not definitely known. Instead of the centrally placed basin-shaped hearth typical of Early Kofun houses, later houses were equipped with a clay "stove" or hooded fireplace which was located in a niche in the center of the wall opposite the entryway. The fireplaces were covered and may have had at least low chimneys (fig. 5.26). Cooking was still done on pedestal stands set in the fire in the "stove." These stands, cooking pottery, and other kitchen equipment were, not surprisingly, almost invariably found on the floor near the fireplace which was thus a clearly defined kitchen area. Sometimes one or two round storage pits were dug into the house floor. If present, these were located on either side of the doorway near the wall opposite the fireplace. The most striking aspect of the Nakada houses is the impression of order and homogeneity they convey.

Given the number of houses found at the site, remarkably few tools and other artifacts were recovered. Iron had apparently replaced stone entirely for cutting tools. Still, iron tools are not abundant and were probably repeatedly re-used. It is also clear that wood was very important in the tool assemblage although no wooden artifacts survived here. Agricultural tools were a very common class of artifacts. Sickles were made by seating a straight iron strap obliquely in a wooden stick. Hoes, shovels, and footplows were of wood but equipped with a socketed iron edge. The iron tips found at Nakada and other sites are similar to Early Kofun and even Yayoi tools, but there appears to have been a general technical improvement through time so that later iron

Figure 5.26. House floor with clay ''stove'' from the Nakada site (courtesy of Atsuko Okada).

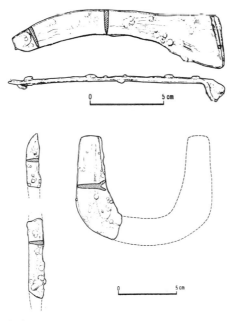

Figure 5.27. Iron tools from the Nakada site. Top, sickle; bottom, knives and slotted shoe for wooden hoe (courtesy of Atsuko Okada).

tools are better made than early ones. The biggest category of Nakada iron artifacts are short knives. Awls, chisels, twist drills, and plane bits were also found, as were several tanged iron arrowheads and larger projectile points. The latter are formally similar to points found as grave goods in tombs and could have functioned either as weapons or hunting tools. Their significance in a domestic site presents a problem of interpretation, since other evidence of hunting is scant. It is unlikely that all of the iron objects found at Nakada were made at the site. One small structure which appears to have been a blacksmith's forge was, however, found in the village. It was less than four meters square and was not as deeply excavated as the pit dwellings. Four large uprights supported the roof, but there is no evidence of walls so that the forge may have been either open or very unsubstantial. In the center was an open hearth which had once been ringed by large rocks. Four fragmented conical clay tubes which are believed to be nozzles for bellows were found near the hearth, and several small scraps of iron were scattered through the ashes. The anvil and all other tools had been removed before the forge had been abandoned. Although it seems clear that iron was being worked at sites like Nakada, this forge is so small and poorly equipped that it appears unlikely it could have been used for a long while. Perhaps small forges like this one were used only briefly by transient smiths or were used by villagers to sharpen or refit old iron tools. The Nakada iron assemblage is fairly representative of Late Kofun iron technology. Tools known from this period but not present at Nakada include saws, axes, adzes, rakes, pitchforks, and fishhooks.

There can be no doubt that the Nakada community drew most of its food from rice agriculture. The situation of the site alone would indicate this. No actual rice grains survived at the site, but spodographic remains of both rice and rice straw were found in the fireplace of at least one house. Broad beans were also cultivated and, besides these, such gathered produce as chestnuts, peaches, acorns, and other wild nuts were also food sources. There is little evidence of hunting or domestic animals.

A very few socio-technic artifacts were found, but these suggest that the canons of taste and perhaps the ideological values of Late Kofun farmers were the same as those of the higher classes. Ornaments recovered from the site include spherical and facetted beads of ground stone and also a number of comma-shaped *magatama* beads. These are similar in form to beads found as grave goods but are not of comparable quality. One disturbed structure at Nakada also yielded a number of crude, fired-clay discs with modeled lugs on one face. These are believed to be imitations of bronze mirrors. If these mirrors had some religious meaning, as has often been suggested, their religious importance does not appear to have been restricted to the elite class, who alone could afford genuine bronze.

We have no sound knowledge of the actual techniques involved in Late

Kofun period wet-rice agriculture. Site situation alone indicates that rice was basic but the techniques of water control, fertilization, and transplantation are unverified. It is possible to assume, however, that all of these steps were practiced, since they were known to Yayoi farmers. The techno-economic bases of Late Kofun culture was therefore apparently much as it had been during the Late Yayoi period. The major changes in the domestic culture were increased availability of iron and improvements in architecture.

Bibliography

Bleed, Peter
    1972. "The Yayoi Cultures of Japan." *Arctic Anthropology* 9 no. 2: 1–23.
Egami, Namio
    1962. "Light on Japanese Cultural Origins from Historical Archeology and Legend." In *Japanese Culture: Its Development and Characteristics*, edited by Robert J. Smith and Richard K. Beardsley, pp. 11–16. Chicago: Aldine.
Hall, John W.
    1965. "The Historical Dimension." In *Twelve Doors to Japan*, edited by John W. Hall and Richard K. Beardsley, pp. 122–184. New York: McGraw-Hill.
Kaneko, Erika
    1966. "Japan." *Asian Perspectives* 8: 24–68.
Kidder, J. Edward
    1964. *Early Japanese Art: The Great Tombs and Treasures.* Princeton: D. Van Nostrand Co.
    1966. *Japan Before Buddhism.* Rev. ed. New York: Praeger.
Komatsu, Isao
    1962. *The Japanese People: Origins of the People and the Language.* Tokyo: Kokusai Bunka Shinkokai.
Pearson, Richard J.
    1969. *Archeology of the Ryukyu Islands.* Honolulu: University of Hawaii Press.
Sugihara, Sosuke
    1961. "The Origin and Growth of the Farming Community in Japan." In *Nihon Noko Bunka no Seisei.* Vol. 1, pp. 1–12. Tokyo: Japan Archaeologists Association.
Tsunoda, Ryusaku, and Goodrich, L. Carrington
    1951. *Japan in the Chinese Dynastic Histories.* South Pasadena: P. D. and Ione Perkins.
Wajima, Seiichi, ed.
    1966. *Nihon no Kokogaku, 3: Yayoi Jidai.* Tokyo: Kawade Shobo Shinsha.

Conclusion

The present lack of good evidence of human activity in Siberia prior to c. 20,000 years ago is disconcerting, but we may with some confidence regard it as a temporary disability. The presence of earlier remains in adjacent areas, the environmental picture, and the undated finds hinting at older inhabitants all point to the conclusion that the record is still far from complete, and that the preceding phases will eventually come to light. We must remember that in the corresponding area of North America we have only the most scanty evidence dating prior to twelve thousand years ago, yet we know it must exist. Archaeology in these northern expanses has scarcely scratched the surface.

Similarly, Pleistocene Siberia as yet contributes nothing specific to the knotty problems of New World origins, beyond providing a fertile field for speculation and for the random pursuit of possible or imagined resemblances in scattered traits. But nothing available is of sufficient age to be relevant, except in terms of possible postglacial cultural diffusion.

However, we can feel that we know enough to conclude that Siberia-Mongolia was not a marginal area during the Pleistocene, but a meeting place of quite different peoples and influences stemming from several directions, with resultant cultural and doubtless genetic interaction, producing a cultural picture that was distinctly its own and not merely a dim reflection of more favored neighbors. We must view it, too, as certainly at times a corridor to the New World, and in all probability as a major hearth as well, though the specifics as yet elude us. As a human habitat, Siberia during glacial times was at least as favorable as Europe, though we have speculated that in the warmer periods the taiga zone may have been shunned and even have served as a barrier. Mongolia in the past was more habitable than it has been subsequently, and seems on present evidence to have been an important source for the populations and cultures of Siberia.

At the close of the Pleistocene an adaptation to forest environments took place which enabled effective exploitation of the taiga habitat, perhaps for the first time. With only a few useful additions from outside such as pottery, ground stone artifacts, and later metal, this pattern and basic technology persisted in much of the forest until relatively recent times. Only on the southern fringe of forest steppe and steppe did new economic patterns eventually take hold. And despite the proximity of a major hearth of cultural dynamism in North China, there was almost total lack of influence from this direction. The Great Wall seems to have been a distinct cultural frontier and barrier long before it came into physical existence.

Japan's geographical isolation is strongly reflected in the cultural record, which is one of indigenous development and minimum outside influence — making the islands an ideal laboratory situation for the student of culture process, though the possibilities have yet to be appreciated. The presence of the oldest presently known pottery in the world (dating back into the terminal Pleistocene) and the problem of its genesis — whether invented or borrowed — remains an enigma. A high level of "forest efficiency" (to borrow a North American concept) was evidently achieved early in postglacial times, which not only displayed stubborn resistance to essential change but provided the milieu for a rich cultural efflorescence, especially in the realm of esthetics. Its ultimate transformation to the farming economy which had swept most of the rest of the arable world was a strikingly late phenomenon, though relatively rapid when it finally occurred. Next to nothing is known as to the identity and source of such outside influences as did impinge on the Japanese islands from the mainland or, conceivably, the Pacific world. But it seems certain that prehistoric Japan exerted no influence on its neighbors, let alone the New World: far-ranging voyagers the Jomon people were not.

Korea's role in prehistoric times seems primarily to have been that of a barrier, not a bridge, between burgeoning China and Japan. Here also agriculture came relatively late, and rice farming inexplicably later still — from whence, is not clear. Much remains to be learned, and scientific archaeology in Korea is in its infancy.

The steppe zone of Inner Asia received its pattern of food production from the west, not from China. Initially this involved farming west of the Yenisei, before the transition to pastoralism. The eastern steppe seems to have moved directly from hunting to herding. Major centers of metallurgy arose in the Altai and in Trans-Baikal, and far-ranging trade and cultural contacts were hallmarks of the steppe peoples, as well as actual population movements. Through this medium, East Asian cultural elements and genes moved westward for the first time, and a number of western traits were received by the early civilization of China.

Perhaps the dominant impression left by such an overview of Northeast Asian prehistory is that of all the world's great hearths of civilization, China (in the times with which we are dealing) exerted the least influence on its immediate neighbors. This situation should pose intriguing problems for the student of culture history and culture process.

Index

Ablation, 136
Acheulean, 12
Achinsk, 26
Adzes: stone, 59, 61, 92, 169, 172; iron, 191, 204
Afanasievo culture, 145
Afontova Gora, 20, 28, 30
Agriculture: in Siberia, 90–91, 93, 96, 145–154 *passim*, 165; in Korea, 104, 105, 166; in Manchuria, 106, 107, 166; introduction of, 114, 139–140, 143, 145, 163–164, 166, 173, 182, 183, 208; in Japan, 114, 117, 128–130, 139–140, 143, 167–170, 173, 175, 182, 183, 185, 195, upland slash and burn, 139, 176; in Inner Mongolia, 163–164, 166; techniques of, 173–174, 175, 178, 204–205; paddy-field, 176. *See also* Irrigation; Millet; Rice; Wheat
Ainu, 100, 102, 143
Alaska, 18
Aleutian Islands, 101
Altai region: environment of, 5; early man evidence in, 11, cultural remains, 18, 20, 153–156, 162, 165–166; metallurgy in, 148, 208; research in, 150; mentioned, 191
Altan-Bulaq, 19*n*
Amur region: environment of, 5, 19; Lower Amur culture area, 82, 91–93; Middle Amur culture area, 82, 86–92 *passim*, 166
Anangula, 38–39, 63
Andronova culture, 148–149
Ang-ang-hsi, 90, 107
Antler, use of, 20, 58, 123, 131
Area Co-tradition, 119–120
Armor, 190, 197, 199–200
Arrowpoints. *See* Bow and arrow
Art: of historical Amur tribes, 92–93; lacquer as medium of, 137; of Okunevo culture, 148; Scytho-Siberian animal style, 148,

156; Haniwa sculptures, 187–188. *See also* Bone art; Figurines
Artic Small Tool tradition,74
Arts-Bogdo, 12–13
Asphalt, 136
Aurignacoid tradition, 19*n*, 20, 38–39, 47, 53
Axes: stone, 59, 61, 87, 89, 92, 123; iron, 191, 204

Baikal region, 74–77 *passim*, 162–163. *See also* Trans-Baikal region
Barley, 139
Basketry, 173
Batons de Commandment, 33
Beads, glass, 189. *See also Magatama*
Beans, 176, 204
Bel'kachi, 65
Bel'kachinsk culture, 65–74 *passim*
Bells, 181
Beringia. *See* Bering Land Bridge
Bering Land Bridge, 10, 18, 38, 44
Big game animals: presence in Siberia of, 3, 8, 11; human exploitation of, 11, 20, 26, 27, 28, 30, 33, 42
Biriusa, 30
Boats, 104, 118, 119, 122, 123, 126–127
Bogdo-Somon, 12
Bone art, 20, 27, 148
Bone tools, 53, 58, 99, 123
Bow and arrow: remains of stone arrowpoints, 37, 58, 79, 87, 89, 92, 98, 107, 123, 128, 169, 172; tanged arrowpoints, 37, 98, 169, 172, 204; remains of bows, 77, 127, 199; portrayed on Haniwa, 197; iron arrowpoints, 199, 204
Bronze: introduction of, 63, 74, 174–175; articles of, 77, 104, 149, 178, 181–182, 189, 190, 192; metallurgy, 148, 149; replaced by iron, 153, 161; production centers, 153, 178–181 *passim*

DESIGNED BY TED SMITH/GRAPHICS

MANUFACTURED BY NORTH CENTRAL PUBLISHING CO.

ST. PAUL, MINNESOTA

TEXT AND DISPLAY LINES ARE SET IN TIMES ROMAN

Library of Congress Cataloging in Publication Data
Chard, Chester S
Northeast Asia in prehistory.
1. Man, Prehistoric — East (Far East) 2. East
(Far East) — Antiquities. 3. Man, Prehistoric — Russia,
Asiatic. 4. Russia, Asiatic — Antiquities. I. Title.
GN855.C27C47   915   73-2040
ISBN 0-299-06430-1